Photoshop Web Magic, Volume 2

D1305938

Photoshop Web Magic, Volume 2

BY JEFF FOSTER

Photoshop Web Magic, Volume 2

Library of Congress Catalog Number: 96-77851
ISBN: 1-56830-392-0

Copyright © 1997 Hayden Books

Printed in the United States of America 1 2 3 4 5 6 7 8 9 0

This book was produced digitally by Macmillan Computer Publishing and manufactured using computer-to-plate technology (a film-less process) by GAC/Shepard Poorman, Indianapolis, Indiana.

Warning and Disclaimer

Trademark Acknowledgments

President Richard Swadley

Associate Publisher John Pierce

Managing Editor Lisa Wilson

Director of Marketing Kelli Spencer

Product Marketing Manager Kim Margolius

The Photoshop Web Magic, Volume 2 Team

Acquisitions Editor
Jawahara Saidullah

Development Editor
Beth Millett

Copy/Production Editor
Michael Brumitt

Technical Editor
Kate Binder

Publishing Coordinator
Karen Flowers

Cover Designer
Aren Howell

Book Designer
Gary Adair

Manufacturing Coordinator
Brook Farling

Production Team Supervisors
Laurie Casey
Joe Millay

Production Team
Trina Brown
Dan Caparo
Kim Cofer
Linda Knose
Kristin Nash

Hayden Books

The staff of Hayden Books is committed to bringing you the best computer books. What our readers think of Hayden is important to our ability to serve our customers. If you have any comments, no matter how great or how small, we'd appreciate your taking the time to send us a note.

You can reach Hayden Books at the following:

Hayden Books
201 West 103rd Street
Indianapolis, IN 46290
317-581-3833

Email address:

Internet: hayden@hayden.com

Visit the Hayden Books Web site at http://www.hayden.com

About the Author

Jeff Foster is an artist/musician of 24 years, where he has been in the forefront of illustrative art and computer graphic design, creating images and effects for clients like McDonnell Douglas, Samsung, Toshiba, Universal Studios, and various motion picture and video special effects houses. His studio has been a beta site for many software companies, including Apple, Adobe, Pixar, Strata, and MetaTools.

He co-authored his first book *Special Edition: Using Photoshop 3.0* (QUE), and has contributed to several other books and magazine articles.

He has lectured and demonstrated his talents and ideas throughout Southern California, and is currently co-developing and teaching a multimedia program for the Dept. of Labor through the North Orange County Community College District.

Jeff also has a software design company, Vicious Fishes™ Software, in Brea, CA., where they are developing a new software category called "Interactive Artware." You can learn more about Vicious Fishes at:

`http://www.viciousfishes.com`

Acknowledgments

My mentors, Kai Krause & Bill Niffenegger, for your sharing of ideas and dreams, and encouraging me to explore my own.

My friends and colleagues who have contributed in part, to this "bleeding-edge" technology of digital imaging: Susan Kitchens, Julie Sigwart, Jeff "Schewbacka" Schewe, Brian Mundy, Mark Lewis, Steve Dodds, Robin Olson, Sam "Yeah-Buddy" Morrison, Ed and Glenn at "spiderprod.com," Robin Rinear, David Palermo, "Hairy" St. Ours, and the cool tools doods at MetaTools. :-)

My literary agent, Brian Gill at Studio B Productions, for your support, encouragement and a good, hearty laugh when I needed it! (uh...your check's in the mail!)

Beth Millett for her encouragement and the rest of the team at Hayden for making this project go together so nicely!

My students at Fullerton College, for their patience and understanding when I fall asleep during a lecture. :-)

My parents, Bob and Pat, thank you for all of your love and support, all of these years!

My "family-in-law," for your support and understanding about the missed family get-togethers. :-)

Oreo the company cat, for keeping me awake all those long nights while writing, and for the furballs in my keyboard. :x

Dedication

For the most important women in the world to me: my wife Cheryl, and my daughters, Jillian, Brittany, and Chelsea. Thanks for your help, patience, and love.

Contents at a Glance

Contents

Introduction

It's a wonderful time to be a web designer. Many new tools and applications can help you look past the programming and move right on to the design work. Yeah, we could all use more bandwidth, faster connections, a terabyte of RAM, and a rich uncle to support our digital habits, but reality dictates that we must keep our web pages clean and lean. Does this mean everything has to be sterile and boring? Hardly!

I've compiled a series of techniques that can be applied in many situations to create truly original "art." You will be able to walk step-by-step through these examples, to create your own, original designs and animations.

Want to start today without having to buy a bunch of third-party filters and applications just to try the examples? You can! All of the techniques in this book are done *entirely* within Photoshop 4.0. Utilizing the built-in Photoshop plug-in filters, combined with various simple painting techniques, you can master the art of creating 2 ½-D images in a few short steps.

Lots of sample images and animations are on the CD-ROM, so you can see how the animations work or the design looks before you dive in. There are several demos and samples of all sorts, as well as the completed effects to review…though I think the cheese puffs and chocolate chips were consumed by the editorial staff! (For more detailed information about what's on the CD and how to access it, check out Appendix C.)

Have fun…and I want to see your homework!

Jeff Foster

Before You Start

Welcome

This book was not meant to be an introductory guide to Photoshop or the World Wide Web. Even if you are new to Photoshop or the web, you will still be able to find lots of useful information. Regardless of your level of experience, this book will help you to build dynamic web graphics with easy-to-follow instructions. If you possess a general understanding of Photoshop but may need the occasional reminder, the Photoshop Basics section will help refresh your memory on fundamental tasks without slowing you down.

System Setup

Adobe recommends 32 MB of RAM allocated to Photoshop 4.0 on Power Macintosh and Windows 3.1, Windows 95, or Windows NT. If you are running a 68030-based Macintosh, Adobe recommends 24 MB of RAM, but I suggest that you add extra memory if you can afford it. The new Photoshop 4.0 filters and other third-party software will push your system to its limits. If you plan to do web design and development professionally, then consider this yardstick. You will be using your system software + Photoshop + HTML editor + word processor + web navigator + fonts + email all open at the same time. Add all these together and you will have a barometer of your memory needs.

Photoshop 4.0 is shipping exclusively on CD-ROM, so it is important that you have a CD-ROM drive. Have lots of storage and consider purchasing at least a two gigabyte hard drive and an alternative external removable drive for back-up. You will be building a large library of pictures and graphics.

All the techniques in this book were created with Adobe Photoshop 4.0 and that's the version I recommend you use. If you're attempting to duplicate these techniques using an earlier version of Photoshop, your results may differ slightly or significantly. If you're working with version 3.0, then you still will be able to create all of the effects in the book. Keep in mind, however, that you will need to adjust the instructions for the differences in the two versions. You will see that even some of the old Photoshop features work differently in Photoshop 4.0. Most of the effects in this book use features that were not available in earlier versions of Photoshop.

Remember to check out Adobe's web site on the World Wide Web. Their URL is http://www.adobe.com. The site is updated frequently and I find it useful for locating information about Adobe products, user groups, and software demos and updates. Adobe also provides a calendar of special events and conferences that they sponsor.

File Size and Download Times

The smaller the file size is, the faster the download time. Remember that one web page may contain several graphic elements and each must download before your web page is completed. Also, don't assume that all web surfers have fast modems. Most people have 28.8 modems, but some still surf from 14.4 modems or may be on a slow LAN. Also, depending on what time of day you're connected (usually between 10 a.m. and 2 p.m. EST), as well as how many people are making hits on a particular site at the same time, you will experience tremendous slow-down periods. If you can manage, make your files 30K or smaller and take advantage of Netscape's and Microsoft's support of layering in their browsers. Layering enables you to build more complex graphics by overlapping several graphic files on top of each other when you download a page. This way you can avoid blank screens.

The Adobe Photoshop 4.0 manual has a detailed chapter on saving and exporting images. Check out the bookmarks list in Appendix A for online resources for finding the most up-to-date information. The web is a perpetually moving target where technical specifications are concerned. Microsoft, Netscape, and other browser developers are continuing to update and change their software. Look for more Java applets and third-party plug-ins for animation, video, and sound.

Conventions Used in This Book

To create graphics in Photoshop for the web you will want to work in RGB mode and set the file resolution to 72 dpi. I've made callouts for each new file, as to what color the background should be. For the sake of clarity, some files you will see here were either developed at twice the size, or zoomed-up to 200% so you can see the details of the examples, though all of the actual sizes are called-out correctly. Also, due to the differences in RGB/CMYK process color production for print, not all of the colors that are called-out, or that you see on the examples on the CD-ROM, will reproduce exactly the same in the printed figures.

The Blue Type

As you work through the steps, you will see phrases that are colored a light blue. The same phrases are listed in alphabetical order in the Photoshop Basics section. If the phrase in blue asks you to perform a task that you are unfamiliar with, you can find that phrase in the Photoshop Basics section, followed by instructions on how to perform that task.

Menu Commands

You will also see instructions that look like this:

Filter➡Blur➡Gaussian Blur (two pixels)

This example asks you to apply the Gaussian Blur filter. To perform this command, click the Filter menu at the top of the screen and drag down to Blur. When Blur is highlighted, a new menu will open to the right from which you can choose Gaussian Blur.

In this example, a dialog box appears that asks you for more information. All of the settings needed to perform each task appear in the text of the instruction step. The preceding example is telling you to enter two pixels as the Radius in the Gaussian Blur dialog box.

Settings

Following each action in the steps are settings for you to use with that feature. These settings are meant to act as guides; the best settings for your web graphic may vary. For starters, begin with the settings that you see in the figures as you proceed through the technique. Unlike monitor calibration used in electronic pre-press, there are no exact references to calibrating your screen to that of the person viewing your web site. As a rule of thumb, if it looks good on your monitor, it will probably work. For example, the following two images demonstrate the importance of adjusting for resolution differences. A five-pixel Radius Gaussian Blur was applied to both images.

Tips

Occasionally in this book you'll also see some paragraphs of text that have been separated out to create Tips, as follows.

TIP **Tips are additional bits of information that can help you render a better effect by providing more information beyond the basic steps of each lesson.**

The 10:00/4:00 Principle

I will often refer you to this simple light and shadow example, or what I call the "10:00/4:00" principle, that will make your objects appear to pop right off the screen. It's an old technique that has been used by the master artists to create volume, mass, and realism, but today it's referred to "2 ½-D", or simulated 3-D.

I've simplified the technique some here, by using the example of a clock face. Imagine that you were to create a sphere, and you were to airbrush a highlight on it in the 10:00 position, as shown in this figure. Notice the white part is applied to the area closest to the 10 on the clock face.

5

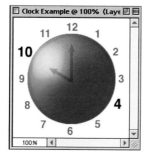
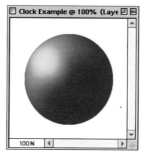

Now you would put a shadow, airbrushed in the 4:00 position. As shown in this figure, the black part is applied to the area closest to the four on the clock face.

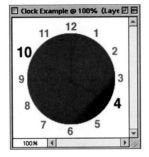 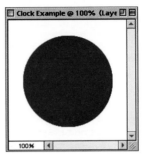

The finished airbrushed highlights and shadows will create the illusion that the "sphere" has dimension.

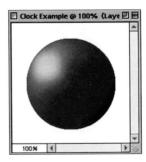

Photoshop Basics

How to Use This Section

This part of the book is intended to help new and novice users of Photoshop with the simple, basic tasks required to do the web graphics we have created. Each of these tasks corresponds to the text highlighted in blue, so users can easily find the instructions they need in this chapter.

This chapter proceeds on two assumptions: that you're creating our web graphics in Photoshop 4.0, and that you're keeping the Tools and Layer/Channel/Path palettes open. If one or both of the Tools and Layer/Channel/Path palettes are closed when you refer to this chapter, you can reopen them by name using the Window menu at the top of the screen. If you're using an earlier version of Photoshop, you can refer to the Photoshop manual for instructions on how to perform these tasks. Also keep in mind that Photoshop 2.5 does not offer the ability to work in layers.

Please note that keyboard shortcuts for Adobe Photoshop for Windows appear between brackets [], and Mac OS shortcuts appear in parentheses ().

The Tools Palette

If you're not familiar with Photoshop's Tools palette, there's no reason to panic. With a bit of experimentation, it doesn't take long to learn each tool's individual functions. Here is the Photoshop 4.0 toolbox.

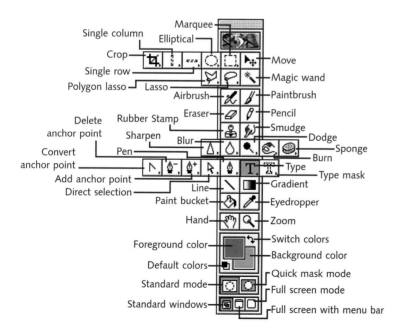

Basic Photoshop Tasks

Add a Vertical/Horizontal Guide

Shortcut: Press (Command-;)[Control-;] to show guides and press (Command-R)[Control-R] to show rulers.

To add a vertical or horizontal guide, choose View➡Show Guides and View➡Show Rulers.

With any tool selected, drag a guide from either the horizontal or vertical ruler. To align the guide with a ruler tickmark, hold down the Shift key as you drag the guide.

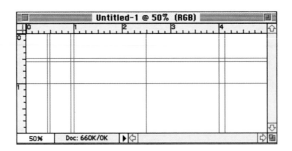

TIP As you drag the guide, hold down the (Option)[Alt] key to switch between horizontal or vertical guides, or vice versa.

Adjust a Layer's Opacity

Drag the Opacity slider in the Layers palette toward the left. If you need to increase the opacity, drag it toward the right.

Convert to a New Color Mode

To convert from one color mode to another color mode, click on the Image menu at the top of the screen and scroll down to the Mode selection, then scroll down in the submenu to select your mode of preference. For example, if you wanted to switch from CMYK mode to RGB mode, you would choose Image➡Mode➡RGB. The checkmark to the left of CMYK will move up to RGB, indicating that the image is now in RGB mode.

 Remember, a different range of colors is available for each color mode. For example, no matter what color mode the file is in onscreen, your printer (if it prints in color) is going to print your work in CMYK. Because the color ranges for RGB and CMYK are different, you should convert your RGB image to CMYK before printing. Otherwise, you may be in for a big surprise when your bright green prints as a dull tan.

Create/Edit a Grid

Shortcut: Press (Command-K)[Control-K] to bring up the Preferences dialog.

To create or edit a grid, choose File➡Preferences➡Guides and Grids, and use the dialog box to set your preferences.

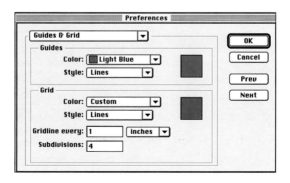

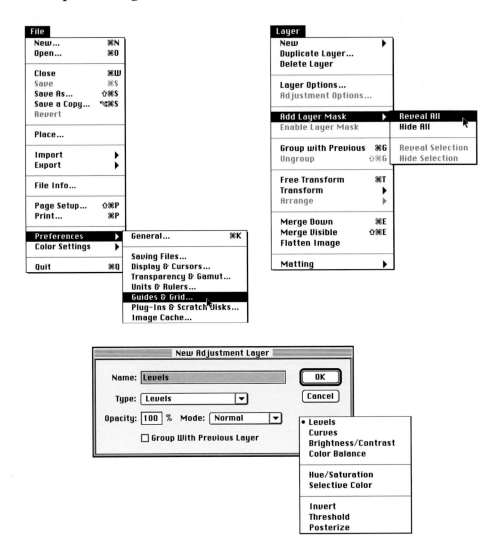

Create a New Channel

Shortcut: Click the New Channel icon or the Save Selection as Channel icon on the Channels palette.

To create a new channel, choose New Channel from the Channels palette menu. To create a new channel from the current selection, choose Select➡Save Selection. The area inside the selection marquee will be white in the channel and the area outside the marquee will be black.

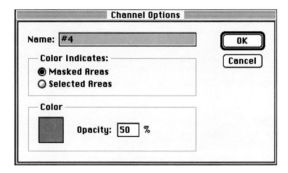

Use the Channel Options dialog box to establish your settings. Unless otherwise noted, I have always used Photoshop's defaults when creating a new channel. This figure shows Photoshop's default settings.

Create a New File

Shortcuts: Press (Command-N)[Control-N].

To create a new file, choose File➡New. The New dialog box appears, where you can name your new file and establish other settings. See "Before You Start" for information on the conventions I used when creating new files for the web graphic examples in this book.

Create a New Layer

Shortcuts: Click the New Layer icon on the Layers palette.

To create a new layer, choose New Layer from the Layer palette menu, or choose Layer➡New➡Layer.

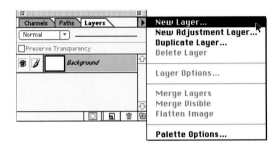

The New Layer dialog box opens, enabling you to name the new layer and establish other settings.

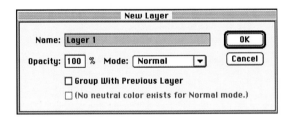

Delete a Channel

To delete a channel, go to the Channels palette, select the channel you want to delete, and drag it to the Trash icon at the lower-right corner—just like you would get rid of a document on the desktop by dragging it to the Trash or the Recycling Bin. You can also select the channel you want to delete and choose Delete Channel from the Channels palette menu.

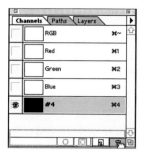 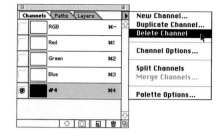

Deselect a Selection

Shortcut: Press (Command-D)[Control-D].

To deselect a selection, choose Select➡None. The marquee disappears. Clicking with a selection tool outside the selection marquee will also deselect a selection.

Duplicate a Channel

Shortcut: Click the channel you want to duplicate, and drag it on top of the New Channel icon on the Channels palette.

To create a duplicate of a channel, make the channel active, then select Duplicate Channel from the Channels palette menu.

13

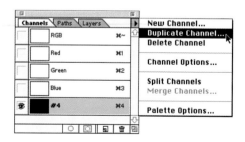

This creates a new copy of the channel you selected for duplication and (if you use the Duplicate Channel command rather than dragging) causes the Duplicate Channel dialog box to appear.

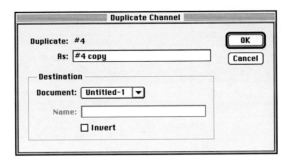

Enter/Exit Quick Mask

Shortcut: Press Q to enter and exit Quick Mask mode.

Click the Quick Mask icon to switch to Quick Mask mode and the Standard mode icon to return to Standard mode.

Essentially a Quick Mask is a temporary channel. When you're in Quick Mask mode, you can use any of Photoshop's tools and functions to change the selection without changing the image. When you switch back to Standard mode, you'll have a new selection.

Enter the Text

There are two type tools in Photoshop 4.0, the standard Type tool and the Type Mask tool. Each effect in this book specifies which type tool to use.

Before entering the text using the standard Type tool, make sure the foreground color is set to the color you want the text to be. The standard Type tool creates a new layer for the type.

The Type Mask tool creates selection outlines of the text you enter without filling them with a new color and without creating a new layer.

To enter the text, select the type tool you want to use, and then click anywhere in the image to open the Type Tool dialog box. Type the text in the large box at the bottom of the dialog box and make your attribute choices from the options above. Unless noted otherwise in the instructions, always make sure you have the Anti-Aliased box checked.

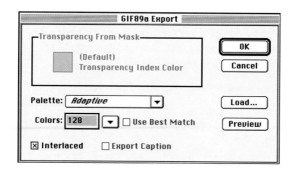

After clicking OK, move the type into position with the Move tool (for regular type) or the Type Mask tool (for type masks).

Export to GIF Format

To export to a GIF format, choose File➜Export➜GIF89a Export. Use the GIF89a format for graphics with transparent areas. In the dialog box choose the Exact, Adaptive, or System Palette (GIF supports a maximum of 256 colors). If you created a custom palette, click Load to locate and select your custom palette. Consult your Photoshop manual or *Designing Web Graphics* by Lynda Weinman for a more detailed discussion of color palette options and the effects they have on file sizes.

The Adaptive palette displays the best results for continuous tone images. Here are two examples (shown in the GIF89a preview window) where the Adaptive palette was limited to 128 colors and 16 colors.

TIP A new alternative to the **GIF** format is the **PNG** format. Unlike **GIF, PNG** keeps all color information in an image and supports alpha channels, as well as using a lossless compression scheme and enabling you to specify how transparent areas will look. Choose File➧Save as➧PNG.

Fill a Selection with Foreground or Background Color

First, set the foreground or background color you wish to use. Keep the selection active and press (Option-Delete)[Alt-Backspace] to fill the selection with the foreground color. If you are in the Background layer, then you can press Delete to fill in the selection with the background color; on a layer, press (Command-Delete)[Control-Backspace] to fill the selection with the background color.

You can also fill in your selections by choosing Edit➧Fill.

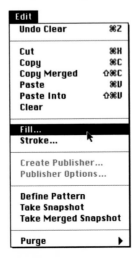

This causes the Fill dialog box to appear, enabling you to establish the Contents option you wish to use, the Opacity, and the Blending Mode.

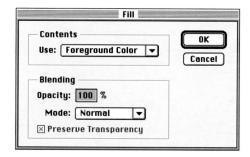

TIP If a selection is empty (a transparent area of a layer) and the Preserve Transparency option is turned on for that layer, you will not be able to fill the selection. To fill the selection, simply turn off the Preserve Transparency option before filling it.

Flatten an Image

To flatten an image (merge all the layers into a single layer), choose Flatten Image from the Layers palette menu or choose Layer➡Flatten Image.

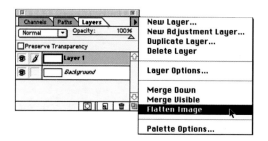

17

Load a Selection

Shortcut: Hold down the (Command)[Control] key and click the channel (on the Channels palette) containing the selection you want to load, or press (Command-Option-channel number)[Control-Alt-channel number].

To load a selection, choose Select➤Load Selection. This brings up the Load Selection dialog box, where you can establish document, channel, and operation variables.

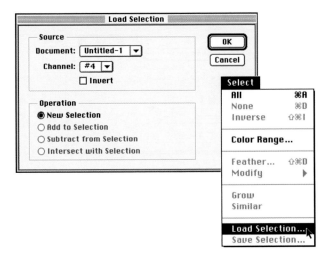

Load the Transparency Selection (of a Layer)

You can load a selection of all non-transparent pixels on a layer—that layer's transparency selection. To load a layer's transparency selection (Command-click)[Control-click] on the layer's name on the Layers palette.

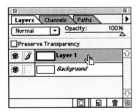

Make a Channel Active

To make a channel active for editing or modification, click on its thumbnail or name in the Channels palette.

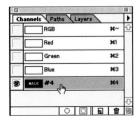

You can tell the channel is active if it is highlighted with a color and its name becomes bold.

Make a Layer Active

To make a layer active, click on its thumbnail or name in the Layers palette.

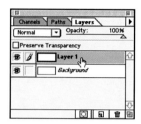

You can tell the layer is active if it is highlighted with a color and its name becomes bold.

Make a Layer Visible/Invisible

To make a layer visible, click in the leftmost column in the Layers palette. If an eye appears, then the layer is visible. If the column is empty, then that layer is hidden (invisible).

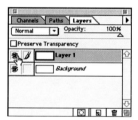
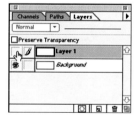

19

Merge Layer Down

Shortcut: Press (Command-E)[Control-E].

To merge a layer with the layer immediately below it, select the layer and then choose Layer➡Merge Down. Remember to check that the layer you wish to merge down into is visible.

Merge Visible Layers

Shortcut: Press (Command-Shift-E)[Control-Shift-E].

To merge visible layers, choose Layer➤Merge Visible. See Make a Layer Visible/Invisible for a review of how to select layers for merging.

Move a Layer

To move a layer, click on the layer you want to move in the Layers palette and drag it up or down along the list of layers to the place you want to move it. As you drag the layer, the lines between the layers will darken indicating where the layer will fall if you let go.

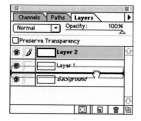

The layer you have moved will appear between layers, numerically "out of order."

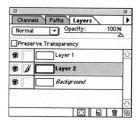

Return to the Composite Channel

Shortcut: Press (Command-~)[Control-~].

If you want to return to the composite channel, click on its thumbnail or name (RGB, CMYK, Lab). The composite channel will always be the one with the (Command-~) [Control-~] after its name.

If you are in an RGB file, then channels 0 through 3 should now be active because the red, green, and blue channels are individual parts of the RGB channel.

Save a Copy

To save a file without losing your previous unedited version, choose File➡Save a Copy. This will bring up the Save a Copy dialog box, where you should name your file and choose a format in which to save it.

This is a particularly beneficial way to save files for an animation sequence, by making a layer visible, and then saving a copy of that file, without destroying or overwriting the data of the original file.

21

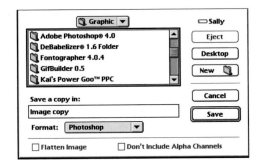

Save a File

To save a new file, choose File➡Save. This will bring up the Save dialog box, where you should name your untitled new file and choose a format and location in which to save it.

To save as another file, choose File➡Save As. This will bring up the Save As dialog box, where you should rename your file and choose a format in which to save it. If a file format that you would like to use is not an option because it doesn't support layers or other Photoshop features you've used in the file, then use the Save a Copy command instead and click on Flatten Layers to make all the formats available.

File format selection is going to depend on what you have in your file, what you want to keep when you save it, and what you're going to do with it afterward. Consult a detailed web site design book, such as *Creating Killer Web Sites* by David Siegel or *Designing Web Graphics* by Lynda Weinman, for more guidance on which file format is best for your needs.

 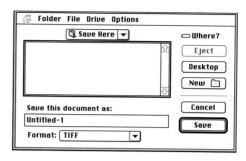

Save as JPEG

To save as a JPEG file format follow the instructions for saving a file. In the JPEG dialog box, experiment with the JPEG settings to find the best result for each photograph. Set the options to maximize image quality while keeping the file size as small as possible.

JPEG (Joint Photographic Experts Group) has become the standard for displaying photographs and other continuous tone images on the web. The JPEG is a lossy compression routine that reduces file sizes without reducing color depth (JPEG supports millions of colors). Because JPEG is a lossy technique, don't resave a JPEG format again as a JPEG. The image will deteriorate.

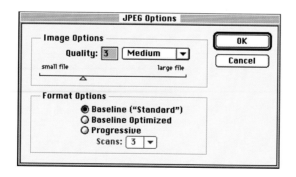

Save a Selection

Shortcut: Click on the Save Selection as Channel icon on the Channels palette.

To save a selection, choose Select➥Save Selection.

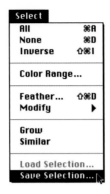

The Save Selection dialog box will open. Choose your desired options and click OK to save the selection.

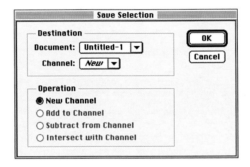

Set the Foreground/Background Color

To change the foreground or background color click the Foreground or Background icon.

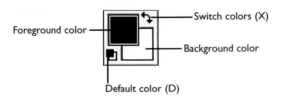

The Color Picker dialog box appears, enabling you to choose a new foreground or background color by moving and clicking the cursor (now a circle) along the spectrum box, or by changing specific RGB, CMYK, or other percentage values. Note that the Foreground and Background icons on the Tools palette now reflect your color choices.

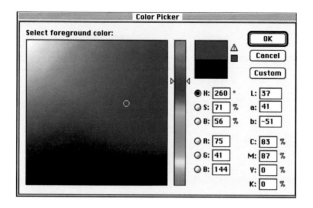

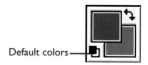

Default colors

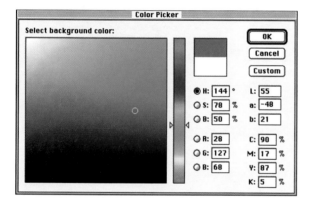

Switch Foreground/Background Colors

Shortcut: Press X to switch the foreground and background colors.

To switch the foreground and background colors, click on the Switch Colors icon. This flips the two colors shown in this icon only and does not affect the image.

25

Switch to Default Colors

Shortcut: Press D to switch to the default foreground and background colors.

If you're on a layer, to change the foreground and background colors to black and white respectively, click on the Default Colors icon. In layer masks or channels, the default colors are white foreground, black background.

Turn On/Off Preserve Transparency

To turn on or off the Preserve Transparency option for a particular layer, first make that layer the active layer. Then, click the Preserve Transparency checkbox on the Layers palette. This option is not available for the Background layer.

PART I

Backgrounds and Tiles

The root of any graphic design layout—whether it's in print, on television or on a web page—is the background texture. Sometimes it's as simple as plain white, with graphic elements softly shadowed above. Sometimes it's a solid color, with clean lines, sharp edges and bold, contrasting text. Sometimes it's a subtle organic texture, with embossed or floating graphic elements. Sometimes it's void of any color at all; the sheer absence of light. Black.

No matter what design concept you choose to portray on your web page, you want to make sure your viewer sticks around long enough to see it in its entirety. Creating a page with impact in this day when WWW stands for the "World Wide Wait" can be a difficult task for designers. This usually means sacrificing the foreground images to have big backgrounds, or vice versa.

Introducing smaller, more efficient, yet visually pleasing background tiles to your web page will empower you as a designer to captivate your audience with less bandwidth. By utilizing the microtiles outlined in this section, your pages will load almost instantly!

Ghosting type into the background image has been a common practice of desktop publishing design for years. Now you can give the illusion of a continuous printed image with no boundaries with this easy-to-create tile.

I Create a new file (128×128, white). Set the foreground color to a desired color. With the Type tool, place some text in the image, being sure not to run off the edges of the page. This will create Layer 1. Repeat with two more text placements on separate layers (Layers 2 & 3), with different foreground colors.

2 Make Layer 1 active and choose Filter➡Other➡Offset (Horizontal: 80, Vertical: 0, Wrap Around). This will make the type on that layer wrap around to the other side of the image window, offsetting it with the other type layers.

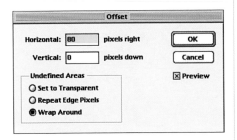

3 Repeat this process on Layers 2 and 3. Create as many layers as you wish, placing type on layers and offsetting the type on each layer at varying amounts horizontally, so none of the text starts/stops in the same vertical alignment. You can also run type over one another for a layered effect if you want, as shown.

4 Flatten the image, then choose Image➡Adjust➡Brightness/Contrast. (Brightness: 50, Contrast: 10). (You can adjust how light/dark you want your text to appear in the background.) This will "ghost" your type tile, enable you to put graphics and text over it, and make a seamless tile when applied to a background.

Check out your new tile by choosing Select➡All, then Edit➡Define Pattern. Create a new file (250×250, white) and choose Edit➡Fill➡ (Pattern, Opacity: 100%, Mode: Normal). You can't tell where the type starts and ends in this image!

29

Microbricks, like Microtiles, are very effective in giving the appearance of being a large, full page image, but are actually very tiny (usually 64 pixels square or less). This effect is a simulated 3D texture, using standard filters and tools in Photoshop 4.0.

1 Create a new file (64×64, white). Set the foreground color to black. Choose View➡Show Rulers and View➡Show Guides. With the Line tool (Width: 2 pixels), draw horizontal lines across the image area from left to right, with a spacing of 32 pixels vertically.

Draw one vertical line, from top to bottom, approximately ⅔ from the left side of the image.

2 Erase the line between the two horizontal lines, as shown, using the Eraser tool (Block, Opacity: 100%). Draw a connecting vertical line between the two horizontal lines, approximately ⅓ from the left side of the image.

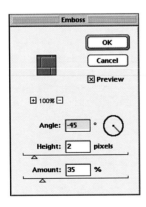

3 Choose Filter➡Stylize➡Emboss (Angle: −45, Height: 2, Amount: 35%). This will give the bricks their depth.

4 Choose Filter➡Noise➡Add Noise (35, Gaussian, Monochromatic). This will add texture to the bricks.

5 Choose Filter➡Blur➡Gaussian Blur (0.3) to smooth out the texture and make it more photorealistic.

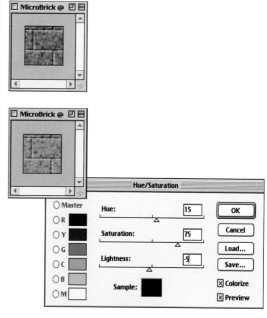

6 Choose Image➡Adjust➡Hue/Saturation (Colorize, Hue: 15, Saturation: 75, Lightness: –5). This will colorize the texture and give it the finishing touch.

7 Check out your new tile by choosing Select➡All, then Edit➡Define Pattern. Create a new file (250×250) and choose Edit➡Fill (Pattern, Opacity: 100%, Mode: Normal). ■

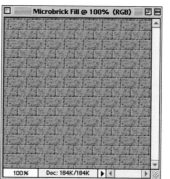

Microtiles are tiny tiling files (typically 16, 32, or 64 pixels square), that load extremely fast on a web page, usually faster than any text. When they are tiled together, they create the illusion of forming one complete page-sized image!

1 Create a new file, (16×16, white). Set the foreground color to a light blue. With the Line tool, draw one horizontal line across the image area from left to right. Draw one vertical line, from top to bottom. (It doesn't have to be exactly in the center, because the tile will repeat itself no matter where you draw the lines.)

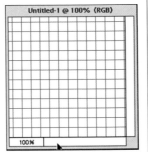

Check out your new tile by choosing Select➡All, then Edit➡Define Pattern. Create a new file, (250× 250) and choose Edit➡Fill (Pattern, Opacity: 100%, Normal). Notice how the tiny microtile has created an effect similar to graph paper, appearing to be the full size of the file!

This microtile is similar in construction, with an added, 3-D embossed effect.

2 Create a new file (16×16, white). Set the foreground color to black. With the Line tool, draw one horizontal line across the image area from left to right. Draw one vertical line, from top to bottom.

3 Choose Filter➡Stylize➡Emboss (Angle: –45, Height: 2, Amount: 35%)

4 Choose Image➡Adjust➡ Brightness/Contrast (Contrast: –75), to give it a smoother texture.

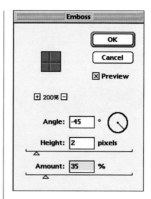

5 Check out your new tile by choosing Select➡All, then Edit➡ Define Pattern. Create a new file (250×250) and choose Edit➡Fill (Pattern, Opacity: 100%, Mode: Normal).

This is a simple, yet effective way to create a ruled page, similar to notebook paper, yet it loads almost instantly before any text appears on the page.

6 Create a new file, (16×16, white). Set the foreground color to medium blue. With the Line tool, draw one horizontal line across the image area from left to right.

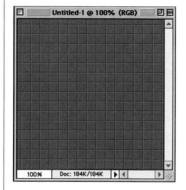

7 Check out your new tile by choosing Select➡All, then Edit➡ Define Pattern. Create a new file, (250×250) and choose Edit➡Fill (Pattern, Opacity: 100%, Mode: Normal).

VARIATIONS

There are literally hundreds of variations you can try with microtiles. An example shown here has a soft shadow beneath the lines, creating the illusion of a "floating grid."

Create a new file (16×16, white). Set the foreground color to a medium gray. With the Line tool, draw one horizontal line across the image area from left to right. Draw one vertical line, from top to bottom.

Choose Filter➡Blur➡Gaussian Blur
(0.5). Set the foreground color to
light blue. With the Line tool, draw
one horizontal line across the
image area from left to right, just
above the blurred horizontal line.
Draw one vertical line, from top to
bottom, just to the left of the vertical line as shown.

Test the tile by choosing Select➡
All, then Edit➡Define Pattern.
Create a new file, (250×250) and
choose Edit➡Fill (Pattern, Opacity:
100%, Mode: Normal). ■

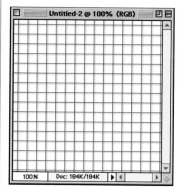

This effect works when tiled down a page, giving the appearance of a spiral notebook in the background. This requires some patience and a few slight adjustments to make sure all of your components line up when tiled.

1 Create a new file (1024×64 white). Choose View➡Show Rulers and View➡Show Guides and View➡Show Grid (set to 8-pixel spacing). Set the foreground color to light blue and draw horizontal lines across the image area from left to right, with a spacing of 16 pixels vertically. Using the rectangular Marquee tool, select an area 16 pixels from the left-hand side, and fill the selection with black, as shown.

2 Create a new layer (Layer 1). Add a vertical guide approximately ¼ inch from the left edge of the "paper." Using the Pencil tool (12-pixel hard-edged brush, Pressure: 100%), carefully paint "holes" equal distance from each other on a vertical guide line as shown. If you mess up on a painted hole, then simply undo the last command and paint it over.

3 Set the foreground color to bright red. Using the Line tool, (Width: 1) draw two parallel vertical lines approximately 1-¼ inches from the left-hand side.

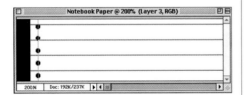

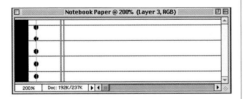

4 Create a new layer (Layer 2). Set the foreground color to a medium gray. Using the Line tool (Width: 3), draw a diagonal line from one of the holes in the paper to just inside the left-hand edge of the image area. Draw a returning diagonal line back toward the next hole, stopping at the edge of the paper. Set the Line tool to Width: 1, and draw over the first diagonal line with a lighter color gray to create the illusion of a highlight as shown.

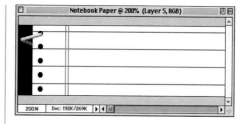

5 Using the Marquee tool, select the lines you just drew and duplicate it by holding down (Option) [Alt] and click-dragging with the Move tool to the next hole in the paper. Repeat for the remaining holes. This may require more adjustments later with the Move tool.

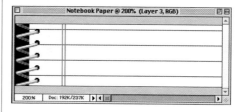

6 Create a new layer (Layer 3) just below Layer 2. Set the foreground color to black. Select the Airbrush tool (17-pixel soft-edged brush, Pressure: 15%) and paint lightly, creating shadows on the edge of the paper beneath each coil. (Since this is on its own layer, you can adjust the opacity if you paint too much shadow!)

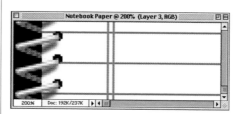

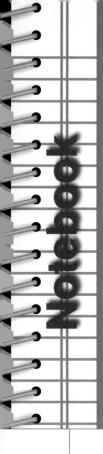

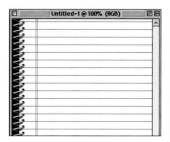

7 Save your tile image (with all of its layers), so you can make slight adjustments to it if necessary. Save a copy of the tile and try it out by choosing Select➡All, then Edit➡Define Pattern. Create a new file, (250×250) and choose Edit➡Fill (Pattern, Opacity: 100%, Mode: Normal). Adjust the alignment of each layer accordingly with the Move tool, and tweak them into place using the arrow keys on the keyboard.

8 When you've made your necessary adjustments and alignments to the layers of your tile, then you're ready to use it in a really unique page design that will make people wonder "how'd you do that?"! ∎

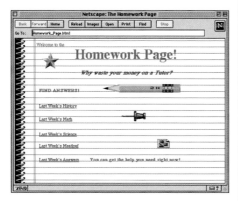

You don't always need to have photos or fancy third-party filters to create great background textures. This sample shows that you can start with a blank image and build a seamless background texture that looks like sandstone using simple techniques and filters built into Photoshop. You can build from that texture to create others, such as Brushed Aluminum and Birdseye Maple as well.

1 Create a new file (128×128, white). Choose Filter➟Noise➟Add Noise (35, Gaussian, Monochrome). This will give us the basic grainy texture for the sandstone. Apply this filter once or twice again to gain density.

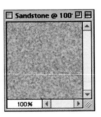

2 Choose Filter➟Blur➟Gaussian Blur (0.5 pixels). This will smooth the texture out a bit to give it a more photographic look.

3 Choose Image➟Adjust➟ Hue/Saturation (Colorize, Hue: 30, Saturation: 50, Lightness: −15) to give your texture some color.

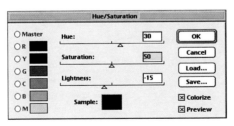

4 Choose Filter➡Noise➡Add Noise (15, Gaussian, Monochromatic). This will add some texture to the tile, to give it an organic feel with some depth. This texture should tile seamlessly because it's created with a random noise pattern and will match without a hard edge.

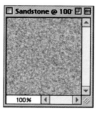

TIP **Check out your new tile's seamless edges by filling a larger image area with the pattern. Choose Select➡ Select All, then Edit➡ Define Pattern.** Create a new file, **(250, 250). Choose Select➡ Select All, then Edit➡Fill (Use: Pattern, Opacity: 100%, Mode: Normal). Notice how the pattern repeats without any hard edges.**

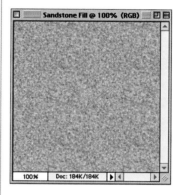

Using the Sandstone texture, you can add a few changes to create a Brushed Aluminum texture.

5 Start with the completed Sandstone texture file opened. To give the base a color resembling aluminum, choose Image➡Adjust➡Hue/Saturation; I used Hue: −100, Saturation: 15, Lightness: −10, but you can adjust it to your own liking.

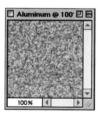

41

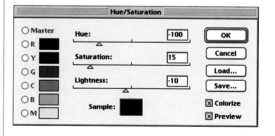

6 Choose Filter➡Blur➡Motion Blur (Angle: 0, Distance: 15). This sets the amount of the "brushing" to the aluminum surface and really brings out the depth in the texture.

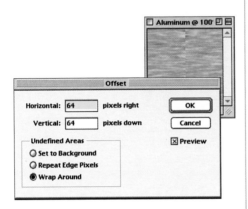

7 To make the texture tile seamlessly, choose Filter➡Other➡Offset (Horizontal: 64, Vertical: 64, Wrap Around).

8 This texture shows a hard edge in only the vertical direction. Double-click the rectangular Marquee tool and set the edge feather to 3. Select an area about ⅓ of the image vertically, including the hard edge that appears. Choose Filter➡Blur➡Motion Blur (Angle: 0, Distance: 10). This will eliminate the line in the middle and create a seamless tile.

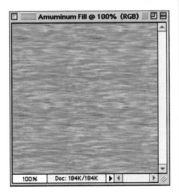

9 To test your new texture for seams, choose Select➡All, then Edit➡Define Pattern. Create a new file, and choose Edit➡Fill (Use: Pattern, Opacity: 100%, Mode: Normal).

42

VARIATIONS

To create a smoother brushed aluminum texture, choose Filter➡ Blur➡Motion Blur (Angle: 0, Distance: 300) at Step 6.

This effect is achieved with only a couple of built-in filters with Photoshop 4.0 and has a nice photographic quality, reminiscent of a piece of fine furniture or an expensive Birdseye maple guitar.

Start with the Sandstone texture file opened. Choose Filter➡Blur➡ Motion Blur (Angle: 45, Distance: 10). This will dictate the direction of the wood grain, so feel free to change the angle to suit your needs.

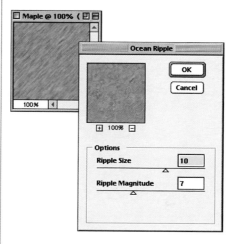

Choose Filter➡Distort➡Ocean Ripple (Size: 10, Magnitude: 7). This gives the texture its maple pattern and glossy finish.

To make the texture tile seamlessly, choose Filter➡Other➡Offset (Horizontal: 64, Vertical: 64, Wrap Around). This texture has hard edges going down the center vertically and horizontally.

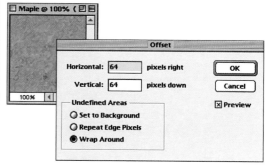

To eliminate the hard edges in the texture, use the Smudge tool (set to three-pixel hard-edged brush, 80% Pressure), and gently smudge across the lines. Be careful to try and blend light areas with light areas; dark with dark.

43

To test your new texture for seams, choose Select➡All, then Edit➡Define Pattern. Create a new file, and choose Edit➡Fill (Use: Pattern, Opacity: 100%, Mode: Normal).

To create a parquet tile pattern using the new texture, use the rectangular Marquee tool to select an area of approximately ⅔ in the center of the texture (hold down the Shift key to keep the selection square) and choose Edit➡Copy. Create a new layer (Layer 1) and choose Paste to apply this selection to a new layer above the background texture. To colorize this layer, choose Image➡Adjust➡Hue/Saturation (Hue: 15, Saturation: 60, Lightness: −15). You may want to change these settings to your liking.

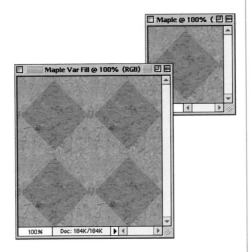

Choose Layer➡Transform➡Rotate (45°). Make sure the layer is centered inside the square of the texture, using the Move tool, and flatten the image. ◼

44

46

Large photo images take forever to download and usually get missed altogether by impatient viewers. One way to assure a nice, large photo on your web site is to create a seamless tile of smaller photos. Many times, web page designers use tiles that have hard edges and aren't seamless and the result is less than appealing.

1 Open the file "Cheese Puffs" included in the WebMagic2/Part 1 folder on the CD-ROM.

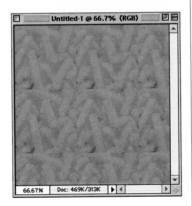

2 If you tile this image as it was originally taken, then we'd get hard edges around each individual tile. This doesn't give the effect of a great amount of cheese puffs, but instead, several small photos of a few puffs.

3 Choose Filter➡Other➡Offset (Horizontal: 80, Vertical: 80, Wrap Around). This will take the hard edges of the outside of the image and bring them into the middle.

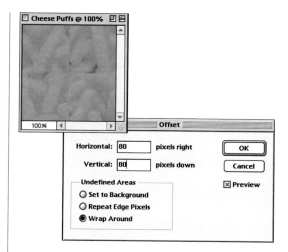

4 Select the Rubber Stamp tool (15-pixel hard-edged brush, 100% opacity). Carefully select areas of the photo that will help you re-create parts of the cheese puffs, and clone over the hard edges down the middle. You will need to take care not to clone too large of an area all at once, or use a soft-edged brush that may cause ghost-ing or a fuzzy image. This may take a few attempts, but have patience if you are new to using the Rubber Stamp tool.

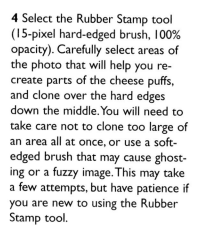

5 Your finished tile should look clean and believable and should tile seamlessly as shown.

47

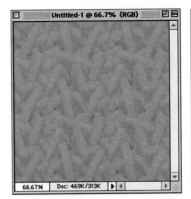

6 Test your newly edited tile by choosing Select➡All, then Edit➡Define Pattern. Create a new file, (250×250) and choose Edit➡Fill (Pattern, Opacity: 100%, Mode: Normal). Now THAT'S a lot of cheese puffs!

7 The possibilities are endless for web page designs using seamless tiled photos in the background.

VARIATIONS

To put a variation of a photo inside a graphic or title on top of a photo tile background, just adjust its opacity or lightness. I started with the tiled image "Chocolate Chips Tile," found on the CD-ROM.

Instead of just lightening the image with the Brightness/Contrast control (which is destructive to the color data in the image), I've opted to duplicate the Background layer (to create Background copy) and fill the Background layer with white. Then adjust the opacity of the image layer (50%) to gain the lightened effect.

You can see here that I've used the lightened photo tile as the background for the type graphics, and it appears to be one solid photo in the web page design. It also makes a tempting, but cruel desktop wallpaper! ■

This effect creates the illusion of a piece of paper with a logo embossed into it. This tiles easily for a background image suitable for any corporate web page.

1 Open up a piece of black and white clip art or a black and white logo design, and resize the image to less than 128×128. By selecting only the black part of the image, copy it to the clipboard. Create a new file (128×128, white). Create a new layer (Layer 1) and paste the contents of the clipboard into it. The white areas of the original artwork are now transparent.

2 Make the Background layer active and choose Filter➡Noise➡Add Noise (Amount: 15, Gaussian, Monochromatic). This will give a bit of texture to the flat white background. Flatten the layers.

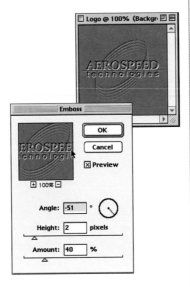

3 Choose Filter➡Stylize➡Emboss (Angle: −51, Height: 2, Amount: 40%). This will give the logo some dimension.

4 Choose Image➡Adjust➡
Brightness/Contrast (Brightness:
100%) to brighten up the image.

5 Choose Filter➡Noise➡Add
Noise (Amount: 10, Gaussian,
Monochromatic). This adds a random rough paper-like texture to
your image so it will tile seamlessly.

6 Check out your new tile by
choosing Select➡All, then Edit➡
Define Pattern. Create a new file,
(250×250) and choose Edit➡Fill
(Pattern, Opacity: 100%, Mode:
Normal). ■

PART II

Borders and Navigation Bars

With HTML, you can only have two "layers" of images occupying the same space at the same time; the background image and the graphics and text you place in the body of the page. What if you want to have the illusion of a large border or "frame" around your floating graphics or text? You usually have to create a large graphic or image map, which takes forever to load, and by that time, you've lost your viewer.

In this section, you will see how to build small graphic borders using tables around your graphics, text, or even your whole page, and still have it load quickly! By creating three to six small inter-linking components, you can build just about any size border or box you want.

Navigational bars can add a unique look and feel to your web pages, as well as provide a clean, easy way to navigate through your site. Using image maps on these simple graphics makes for easy navigation, and combining these techniques will definitely get your web site noticed!

You can create a huge "marquee" with only four animated GIF files that are less than 11K each! This effect gives the illusion that you have a string of flashing arrows chasing around in a clockwise loop. You can also use this effect as a chasing divider rule.

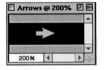

1 Create a new file (64×16, black). Create a new layer (Layer 1) and set the foreground color to a bright yellow-orange from the Scratch palette. With the Line tool (Width: 4, Anti-aliased, Arrowheads: Start), click-drag a small arrow in the center of the image as shown.

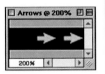

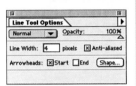

2 Duplicate Layer 1 (Layer 1 copy). Using the Move tool, move the arrow to the right of the center arrow as shown. (Hold down the Shift key to lock image into the horizontal direction while moving.)

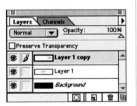

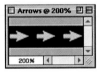

3 Duplicate layer copy (Layer 1 copy 2). Using the Move tool, move the arrow to the left of the center arrow as shown.

4 Make Layer 1 copy active. Adjust the opacity to 50% and select Hard Light from the pull-down menu on the Layers palette. Repeat on Layer 1 copy 2. This will give the appearance that the arrows are "unlit."

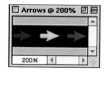

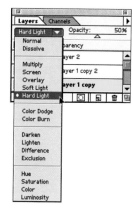

5 Hide all layers except for the Background layer. Create a new layer (Layer 2). Choose View➡ Show Brushes to bring up the Brushes palette. Choose Load Brushes from the Brushes palette menu and locate the Assorted Brushes file. Select the small "starburst" brush (Pressure: 11%) and click two or three times in the center of the image.

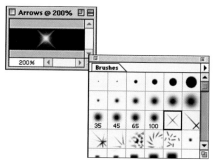

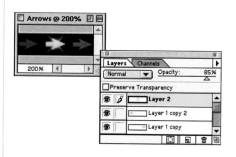

6 Make all layers visible. Set the opacity of Layer 2 so you can see the center "lighted" arrow through it (approximately 75–85%). This will give the effect that the light is emitting a glistening light. Export as GIF89a. Name the file "top1.gif," as it will be the first frame of a three-frame sequence.

7 Reset the settings on Layer 1 copy (100%, Normal), and set Layer 1 to 50%, Hard Light. Make Layer 2 active and use the Move tool to move it over the arrow on Layer 1 copy. Export as GIF89a and name it "top2.gif."

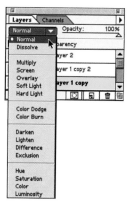

8 Reset the settings on Layer 1 copy 2 (100%, Normal) and set Layer 1 copy to 50% and Hard Light. Make Layer 2 active and move it over the arrow on Layer 1 copy 2 with the Move tool. Export as GIF89a and name it "top3.gif."

9 Open the file named top1.gif that you created in Step 6. Choose Image➡Rotate Canvas➡90° CW. Save as "down1.gif." Repeat with image files top2.gif and top3.gif, saving and renaming them accordingly.

10 Open the file named down1.gif that you created in Step 9. Choose Image➡Rotate Canvas➡90° CW. Save as "bottom1.gif." Repeat with image files down2.gif and down3.gif, saving and renaming them accordingly.

11 Open the file named bottom1.gif that you created in Step 10. Choose Image➡ Rotate Canvas➡90° CW. Save as "up1.gif." Repeat with image files bottom2.gif and bottom3.gif, saving and renaming them accordingly.

12 Assemble your frames in GifBuilder or GIF Animator in the order that you named them, making sure to set "Loop Forever" for each animation. You will have four separate animated gif files that can be linked together inside separate table cells in your HTML editor. The final result is really eye-catching!

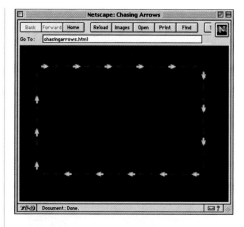

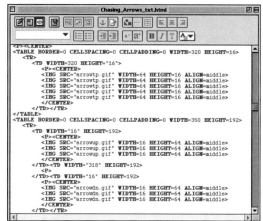

You can try this animation sample located in the WebMagic2/Part IV folder on the CD-ROM. ▪

57

Who says you have to use a 3D application or third-party plug-ins to create realistic 3D graphics for your web site? This effect creates a beautiful, glossy control strip that comes apart in three sections. You can add any color or texture imaginable and have as many sections as you want. This type of graphic shape can be used for an imagemap or for rollovers.

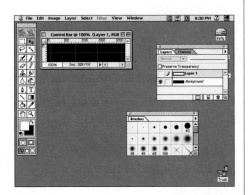

1 Create a new file (250×50, black). Add a horizontal guide centered in the image. Add four vertical guides, two placed 10 pixels from each end, and the other two 80 pixels from each end.

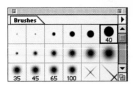

2 Create a new layer (Layer 1) and set the foreground color to white. Double-click the Paintbrush tool and bring up the Brushes palette. Edit a hard-edged brush using the Brush Options (by double-clicking a paintbrush) and create a 40-pixel brush. Make sure your paintbrush cursor preferences are set to Show Brush Size. Click the right side of the far-left guides. Hold down the Shift key and click the left side of the far-right intersection of guides. This creates the basic outline shape, though you may wish to create a thinner or wider shape by using a different sized brush.

3 Create a new layer (Layer 2). Set the foreground color to black. Create a 30-pixel hard-edged brush, using the Brush Options. With the Paintbrush tool, carefully click the center of the left radiused edge of Layer 1 below. Hold down the Shift key and click inside the center of the right radiused edge. This will create the basic shape of the 3D bar, inside of a 5-pixel border.

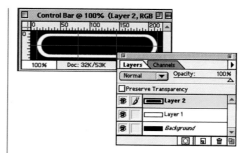

4 Load the transparency selection of Layer 2 and choose Select➡ Modify➡Contract (four pixels). Then choose Select➡Feather (two pixels).

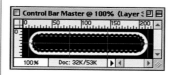

5 Choose Select➡Inverse. Using the Magic Wand (Tolerance: 1), hold down (Option)[Alt] and click in the outside area to deselect up the edge of the image. This will keep the selection confined to the inside of the black ellipse, with feathering on the inside. Create a new layer (Layer 3).

6 Set the foreground color to white. Select the Airbrush tool (Pressure: 11%, 12-pixel soft-edged brush). Click in the top-right corner of the selection. Hold down the Shift key and click the top-left corner of the selection. (Make the selection invisible to help see the details more easily.) Carefully paint along the left edge (10:00 position) to create a soft highlight. Repeat until desired highlight strength is achieved.

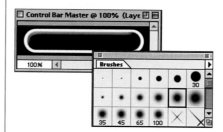

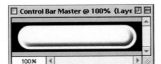

7 Make Layer 2 invisible and set the foreground color to black. Continue the airbrush process on Layer 3, working along the bottom-right edges (4:00 position) to create a soft shadowed effect. When desired effect is achieved, deselect the selection.

8 Make Layer 1 invisible and load the transparency selection of Layer 2. Create a new layer (Layer 4) directly beneath Layer 3. Set the foreground color to a medium gray and fill the selection, then hide the layer. You can use this to modify the colors of the control panel graphic later.

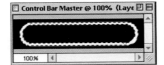

9 Load the transparency selection of Layer 2. Make Layer 1 active and delete the selection. Load the transparency selection of Layer 1.

10 Choose Select➡Modify➡ Contract (one pixel), then choose Select➡Feather (1 pixel). Create a new layer (Layer 5). Set the foreground color to white and fill the selection. Deselect and hide Layer 1. This will be the rounded ring around the control bars.

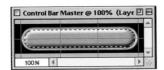

11 Make Layers 3, 4, 5, and the Background visible. Create a new layer (Layer 6). Select View Guides and double-click the Line tool to bring up the Line Tool Options palette (width: 1 pixel, Anti-aliased). Set the foreground color to a medium gray. Load the transparency selection of Layer 4 and draw one line down each of the center vertical guides. This will be where the control bars split apart.

12 Make the guides invisible and deselect. Set the Layer Options to Darken, with the Preserve Transparency option selected. Use the Dodge/ Burn tool to lighten the top of the vertical lines and darken the bottom ends of the lines. This will give the illusion that the bars actually "divide" along these lines.

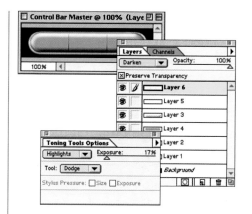

VARIATIONS

Several color schemes and textures can be created from this basic control bar master. To create a deep woodgrain effect, follow these next steps.

Duplicate Layer 4 (Layer 4 copy) and position the new layer above Layer 4, with Preserve Transparency selected. Choose Filter➡Noise➡ Add Noise (20, Gaussian, Monochrome).

Choose Filter➡Blur➡Motion Blur (Angle: 5°, Distance: 10) to create the woodgrain texture.

Choose Image➡Adjust➡ Hue/ Saturation (Colorize, Hue: 15, Saturation: 75, Lightness: -40). This will give the wood a deep, rich color and texture.

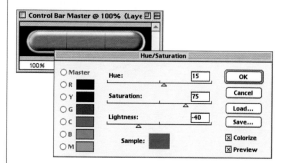

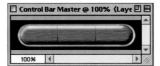

To bring out the details in the woodgrain texture, choose Filter➡ Sharpen➡Unsharp Mask (200%, Radius: 1).

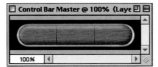

As not to over-power the beautiful woodgrain texture, set the opacity of Layer 3 down to approximately 60%. This will give the texture a more believable appearance.

Brass Edges

To add a brass color to the outside rim, duplicate Layer 5 (Layer 5 copy) and position the new layer above Layer 5. Choose Image➡ Adjust➡Hue/Saturation (Colorize, Hue: 40, Saturation: 75, Lightness: -45).

Choose Filter➡Sharpen➡Unsharp Mask (100%, 1) to clean up the edges and make the rim appear brighter and shinier.

Charcoal Texture

To create a slick charcoal-black texture, hide all layers (except for Layer 5 copy, Layer 3 , Layer 4, and the Background layer). Make Layer 4 active and set the opacity to approximately 20%.

Now to dice up these bars into separate pieces.

Choose View➡Show Guides and select the Crop tool. Drag the Crop tool from the top right-center vertical guide line down to the bottom-right corner, as shown.

Choose Save a Copy (Flatten, JPG) and name it "controll.jpg." Choose File➡Revert on the master file and crop the center section between the two vertical guide lines. Save a copy and name it "controlc.jpg." Continue with the third selection and name it "controlr.jpg." This will give you three control bar components that you further modify and add type to, if desired.

To add text to the control bars, set the foreground color to a light, contrasting color (I chose white for this example). Place and center text over the middle portion of the bar. Set the Opacity down to approximately 70% to blend in with the bar texture.

You can have as many bars lined-up in a row as you want, each having a different URL link attached. ■

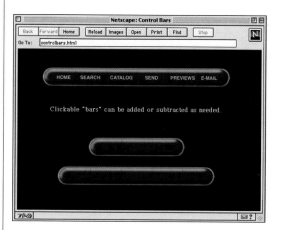

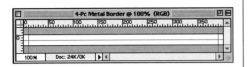

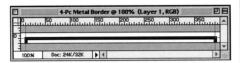

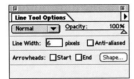

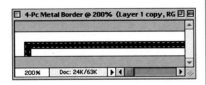

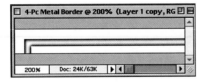

This effect has a nice metallic look and it's created in only three parts. Your viewers will swear it's a full-sized background image! The completed files are small and can be made to fit any size page you wish to border or divide.

1 Create a new file (400×20, white). Select View Rulers. Add a horizontal guide in the middle of the image. Add two vertical guides, 10 pixels in from each end.

2 Create a new layer (Layer 1). Set the foreground color to black and double-click the Line tool and set the Line Width to 6 and turn Anti-aliased off. Draw a line from the left guide intersection to the right intersection. Next, draw a line on the left, from the top of the horizontal line down, out of the image area. Repeat on the right side.

3 Hide the guides and rulers. Duplicate Layer 1 (Layer 1 copy). Load the transparency selection of Layer 1 copy and choose Select→Modify→Contract (1 pixel). Choose Select→Feather (one pixel).

4 Set the foreground color to white and fill the selection. Deselect. This will give the bar a 3D rounded appearance.

5 Choose Image➡Adjust➡Hue/
Saturation (Colorize, Hue: –115,
Saturation: 20). This will give the bar
a metal color, similar to polished
aluminum.

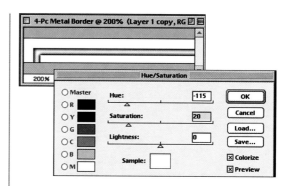

6 Zoom in on the corner of the
image. Using the Block Eraser tool,
remove the corner three pixels off
each corner. This will give a more
rounded appearance when reduced
back to normal.

> **TIP** It's easier to see if the pix-
> els are really removed if
> you hide the layers below
> the one you're working on.

7 Make Layer 1 active. Choose
Filter➡Blur➡Gaussian Blur (2.0
pixels). This will be the shadow
layer.

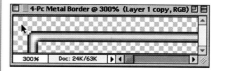

8 Set the opacity of Layer 1 to
50%. With the Move tool selected,
use the arrow keys to nudge Layer
1 down two pixels and to the right
two pixels, to create the proper
positioning for the drop shadow.
This will be the first piece to the
frame. Choose File➡Save a Copy
(Flatten Image, JPEG) and name it
"top.jpg."

9 Select Image➡Rotate
Canvas➡Flip Vertical. With the
Move tool selected, use the arrow
keys to nudge Layer 1 down four
pixels. This should position the
shadow correctly, but it leaves a
white gap at the top edge.

65

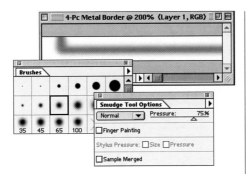

10 Make Layer 1 copy invisible. Double-click the Smudge tool and set its Pressure to 75%. Choose a 7-pixel soft-edged brush and carefully smudge the shadow up to fill in the gap at the top on each side. Make Layer 1 copy visible and choose File➡Save a Copy (Flatten Image, JPEG), naming it "bottom.jpg."

11 Choose Image➡Rotate Canvas➡90°CCW to put the image in an upright position.

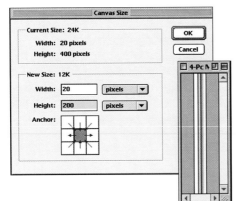

12 Select Image➡Canvas Size and set it to 20×200. Click Proceed. The dialog box warns you if the image will be clipped. This will crop the ends off the bar. Choose Save a Copy (Flatten Image, JPEG) and name it "sides.jpg." You will use this same image for both the left and right sides of the frame.

TIP You may wish to use a smaller vertical sized side bar, in which case you would simply crop tighter on the height. You can then "stack" the bars on top of each other in your **HTML** editor to gain the desired final effect.

13 Open your HTML editor and create a file with a white background. Insert the image "top.jpg" inside a one-row, one-cell table, centered with no border. Without a return, create a one-row, three-cell table, centered, no border. Insert the image "sides.jpg" in each of the two outside cells. Set the cell size to that of the images. Without a return, create another one-row, one-cell table, centered, no border, and insert the image "bottom.jpg." You can put whatever text or graphics you want in the center cell of the middle table.

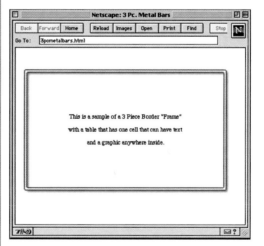

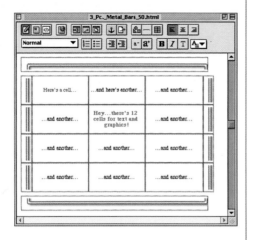

VARIATIONS

Another way to take advantage of the smaller vertical bars is to replace the middle one-row, three-cell table, with a four-row, five-cell table (or more if you want). Shown here inside the window of our HTML editor, so you can see the actual table components, and then in Netscape Navigator.

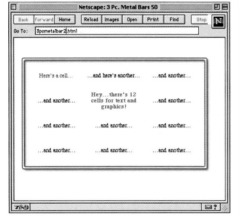

If you'd like your bars to have a transparent background to put over another texture (no shadow), then these simple steps will help you quickly!

Open the master document and make Layer 1 copy active. Hide all other layers, and export to GIF89a. The background will be transparent automatically. Repeat for the other two files.

The transparent images will overlay seamlessly on top of any background texture, giving the illusion that it's all one big image file with the border rendered into it!

You can get the above HTML text from the Borders & Rules folder on the CD-ROM. ■

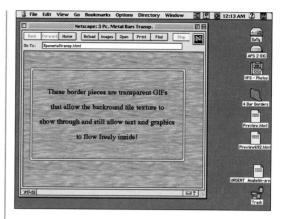

Want to put large borders around tables or have several dividers or rules on your page, but don't want to burden the download time? These little balls can be "stitched" together in a string to create interesting borders or dividers...and it's less than 11K in size!

1 Create a new file (16×16, black). Choose View➤Show Brushes and create a 12-pixel hard-edged brush, then choose the Paintbrush tool.

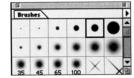

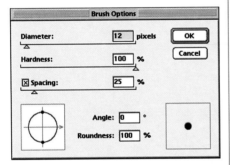

TIP When working on small images such as this, it's best to view them at 200%. Sure, it doesn't look as nice, but you'll have much better control and be able to see what you're doing easier!

2 Create a new layer (Layer 1). Set the foreground color to a desired base color (I used an aqua green). Click in the center of the image and turn on Preserve Transparency. This will serve as the base of the 3D ball against a solid background.

3 Create a new layer (Layer 2). Using the Pencil tool and the same size brush, click in the center of the image. Turn on Preserve Transparency. This will create an aliased-edged for a transparent GIF to use with a textured or colored background.

4 Select the Airbrush tool (Pressure: 11%, seven-pixel soft-edged brush). Set the foreground color to white. Lightly airbrush the top-left corner of the ball (10:00 position). Just a couple clicks of the mouse will do. This will create the highlight area of the sphere.

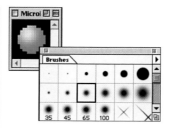

5 Set the foreground color to black and the brush size to a five-pixel, soft-edged brush. With quick, short strokes of the airbrush, gently darken the bottom-right edge of the ball (4:00 position). This will give a slight shadow to the ball, completing the 3D effect. Make the background layer invisible and export to GIF89a (Adaptive, 216 colors). The transparent background will automatically be converted for you. Now you can place this ball over any kind of background texture.

6 To create a ball with anti-aliased edges, make Layer 2 invisible. Make Layer 1 active and repeat Steps 4 and 5 on this ball. Choose Save a Copy and select JPEG format. This will be easily imported into your HTML editor for multiple occurrences on your web page. You may also choose to export as GIF89a.

71

Variations

You can create virtually any colored balls you'd like after the first one is completed. This variation will create a gold colored anti-aliased ball on a black background.

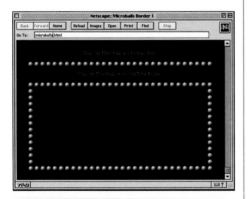

Duplicate Layer I and choose Image➤Adjust➤Hue/Saturation (Colorize, Hue: 35, Saturation: 85, Lightness: 10). Save or export your images accordingly.

Here are some samples of the kinds of borders, dividers, and designs you can create with these little balls. Remember, they're less than 11K and only load *once* on your web page! ■

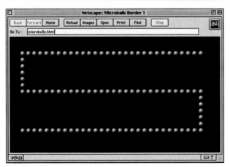

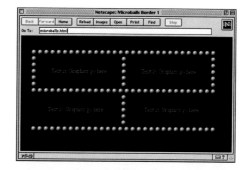

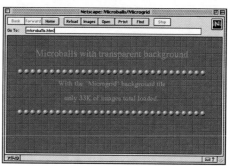

This is an exciting time for the Internet with the ability to put Shockwave movies or QuickTime and QuickTime VR movies on your web pages. The only problem is presenting them so they don't look like they're just stuck there in space. Here's a nice way to frame your movie and have it blend in with the background texture (works great with still images too). We'll create a frame and then cut it apart to "frame" your movie with in the HTML editor.

I Create a new file the exact size of your QuickTime or Shockwave movie file (mine was 320×200). Duplicate the background layer (Background copy). We'll use this as a template to work around.

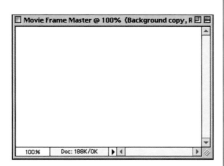

2 Set the background color to black. Choose Image➡Canvas Size and set your image 32 pixels larger in height and width than your original, making sure the center position box is selected. This will give you a 16-pixel frame around your movie. (If you want a larger frame, then start with a larger number.)

3 Open a seamless background texture file (I used Granite Texture, found in the WebMagic2/Part I/tiles folder on the CD-ROM). Select All and choose Edit➡Define Pattern. For this example, I want the edges of the frame to disappear when against the background texture, so the tile I'm using is a random pattern, "organic" texture.

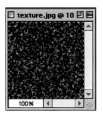

4 Make the Background copy layer invisible and make the Background active. Choose Edit➡Fill (Pattern, 100% Normal). This will fill the background with the texture you selected.

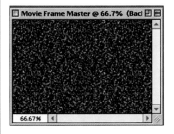

5 Make the Background copy layer visible. Select View Rulers and add guides along all four sides of the white rectangle on the Background copy layer.

6 Make the Background copy layer invisible. Select the Burn tool (Midtones, Exposure: 50%, 13-pixel soft-edged brush). Click the upper-left guide intersection. Hold down the Shift key and click the upper-right guide intersection. This will create a "indentation" in the texture; the more you apply the Burn tool, the more depth will be applied. Continue in a clockwise direction all the way around, until the desired "depth" is achieved.

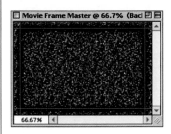

7 Make the Background copy layer visible to see if the alignment is accurate. It should appear that the white panel is slightly sunken into the background texture.

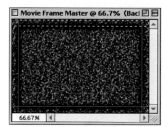

8 Make the Background copy layer invisible. Using the rectangular Marquee tool, select the area from the top horizontal guide to the top of the image. Copy the selection to the clipboard.

9 Create a new file, leaving the default settings that appear in the dialog box. Paste your selection in (this creates Layer 1). Flatten the image and save as a JPEG (JPG) file or export as GIF89a. (Make sure to name your file "top.jpg" or something that will be distinguishable when you're assembling the frame in your HTML editor.)

10 Using the rectangular Marquee tool, select the area on the right side of the right vertical guide, under the top guide and all the way to the bottom. Copy the image to the clipboard and repeat Step 9. Do the same for the left side of the image.

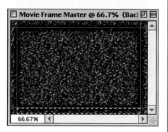

11 Using the rectangular Marquee tool, select the area on the bottom side of the bottom horizontal guide, between the two vertical side guides. Copy the image to the clipboard and repeat Step 9.

12 You will have four separate files, which should be named according to their position in the frame for easier assembly in your HTML editor.

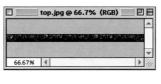

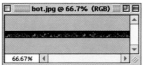

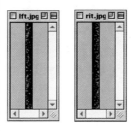

13 Using your HTML editor, apply your matching background texture to the page. Position the "top.jpg" piece of the frame inside its own one-row, one-cell table, centered and no border. Without using a return, create a new one-row, three-cell table with no border. Insert your "left.jpg" and "right.jpg" images into the outside cells and adjust the cell size accordingly. Embed your movie file into the center cell, choosing no controller. Without using a return, add your "bottom.jpg" image into the center cell right under the movie image, centered.

14 The finished page beautifully frames your movie file. You can find the sample file in the WebMagic2/ Part II folder on the CD-ROM. ■

77

ORDER
INDUSTRY
LINKS
CUSTOMERS
SERVICES
PRODUCTS
SEARCH

78

One effect that seems to be sweeping the web is graphics that act as imagemaps, transporting you to other locations with just a rollover and a click. This effect can be done easily, and once you have the hang of it, the variety of shapes, sizes, and textures can be endless.

I Create a new file (400×128, black). Select View➡Show Rulers and add a horizontal guide anywhere down the middle of the image area. Add two vertical guides, approximately 30 pixels from each end.

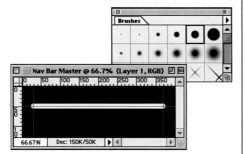

2 Create a new layer (Layer I), and set the foreground color to white. Using the Paintbrush tool (Pressure: 100%, 13-pixel hard-edged brush), click the intersection of the left guides. Hold down the Shift key and click the intersection of the guides on the right.

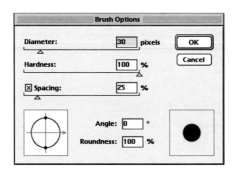

3 Choose View➡Show Brushes to open the Brushes palette. Double-click the largest hard-edged brush in the top row to open the Brush Options dialog box. Change the diameter of the brush to 30 pixels. Click OK.

4 Add a vertical guide approximately 150 pixels from the left. Using the new 30-pixel hard-edged brush, click the intersection of the guides you added. Hold down the Shift key and click the intersection of the guides on the left. This will give you the basic shape of your navigation bars.

5 Duplicate Layer 1 (Layer 1 copy). Using the Move tool, separate the images vertically.

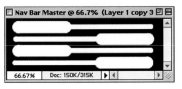

6 Duplicate Layer 1 copy twice more (Layer 1 copy 2, Layer 1 copy 3). On each of the new copies, choose Layer➡Transform➡Flip Horizontal. Use the Move tool to evenly space all of the images within the main image area.

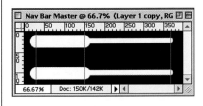

7 Merge all layers, except for the background layer. Rename the merged layer "Nav bar." Make the Nav bar layer active and select all and copy to the clipboard. Delete the Nav bar layer.

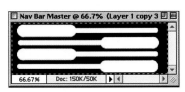

8 Create a new channel (Channel #4) and paste.

9 Return to the composite channel. With the selection still active, create a new layer (Layer 1).

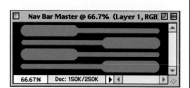

10 Set the foreground color to a medium gray and fill the selection.

11 With the selection still active, choose Select➡Modify➡Contract (three pixels). Then choose Select➡Feather (two pixels). Invert the selection.

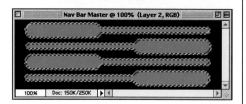

12 Using the Magic Wand tool (Tolerance: 1), hold down the (Option) [Alt] key and click in the black area to deselect the outer area of the image. This will give a clean edge on the outside of the bars and a soft inner selection.

13 Create a new layer (Layer 2). Set the foreground color to white. Hide the selection. Using the Airbrush tool (Pressure: 11%, 9-pixel soft-edged brush), carefully paint highlight areas along the top edges and over to the right (10:00 position). This can be done by clicking the left end of a horizontal edge and holding down the Shift key, and clicking the right end. Repeat until the desired highlight strength is achieved (I applied three times with the previous settings).

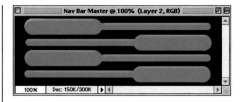

14 Set the foreground color to black and apply similarly to the bottom edges and up the right sides (4:00 position). Apply until the desired amount of shadow is achieved.

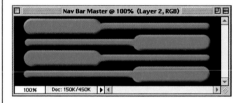

VARIATIONS

Now that there's a base to work from, we can make several variations from it, even adding textures and text!

Make Layer 1 invisible and load the transparency selection of Channel #4. Set the foreground color to white. Create a new layer (Layer 3) just above the Background layer and fill the selection. Adjust the opacity of Layer 3 to approximately 25%. This will create a gray plastic look.

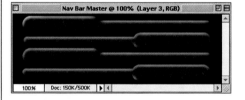

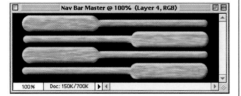

Adding Texture

Open the Aluminum Tile file in the WebMagic2/Part I/tiles folder on the CD-ROM. Select all and choose Edit➛Define Pattern. Return to the master file, and create a new layer (Layer 4) just above the Background layer. Load the transparency selection of Channel #4 and fill the selection (Pattern, 100%, Normal). This will create a nice brushed aluminum look to the bars. You can add virtually any seamless texture to these bars.

Adding Text

To add text to your navigation bars, simply use the Type tool with a contrasting foreground color, which creates a new layer at each insertion. Center and position your type directly over the bars with the Move tool, and adjust the layer opacity to achieve the desired effect. Save the images entirely as JPEG (JPG) files and add the image map "hot spots" in your HTML editor. You can also export them to GIF89a with or without transparency. So experiment and have fun! ■

You can take virtually any tiled image and overlay highlights and shadows to create a 3D effect. In this effect, we create a 3D "frame," complete with mitered corners, which can be easily modified and manipulated into different layouts.

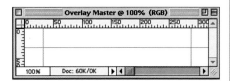

1 Create a new file (360×64, white). Select View➡Show Rulers and add a centered horizontal guide. Add two vertical guides, approximately 32 pixels from each end. (Of course, you can adjust these sizes to suit your needs.)

2 Create a new layer (Layer 1), and set the foreground color to black. Using the Line tool (Width: 32), draw a line from approximately 16 pixels to the left of the intersection of the guides, to 16 pixels to the right of the intersection on the right.

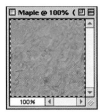

3 Open a seamless background texture file (I used Maple Texture, found in the WebMagic2/Part I/tiles folder on the CD-ROM). Select all and choose Edit➡Define Pattern.

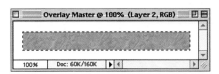

4 Load the transparency selection of Layer 1 and create a new layer (Layer 2). Fill the selection (Pattern, 100%, Normal).

5 Choose Select➡Modify➡ Contract (six pixels). Then choose Select➡Feather (three pixels).

6 Choose Select➡Inverse. Double-click the Magic Wand tool and set the tolerance to one pixel. Hold down the (Option)[Alt] key and click in the white area (outside the active image area). This will give you a selection that is hard-edged on the outside of the bar and soft in the middle.

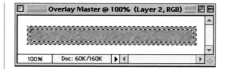

7 Create a new layer (Layer 3). Double-click the Airbrush tool to set the options (Pressure: 8%). Set the foreground color to white. Using a 9-pixel soft-edged brush, click in the upper-right-hand corner of the selection area. Then hold down the Shift key and click in the upper-left-hand corner of the selection, and then click again down to the lower-left side of the selection. Repeat until the desired strength of the highlight is achieved. (Hide the selection to see the image you're working on more easily, without deselecting the selection.)

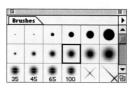

8 Set the foreground color to black and repeat Step 7 along the bottom and right edge of the selection until the desired shadow strength is achieved. Merge down to Layer 2 to combine the highlights/shadows with the texture. Deselect.

9 Duplicate Layer 2 (Layer 2 copy). Choose Layer➡Transform➡Rotate 90° CCW. Using the Move tool, move the image down and to the right until the top right corner matches up with the image below.

85

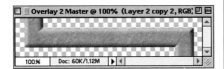

86

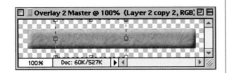

10 Using the polygon Lasso tool (Anti-aliased), hold down the Shift key and select a perfect 45°angle across the overlap of the two images, creating a selection for a "miter joint" between the two.

11 Delete the selection and deselect. The result should be a perfect miter joint that even your dad could be proud of.

12 Duplicate Layer 2 copy (Layer 2 copy 2). Using the Move tool, move the image over to the left side and align its left side with the end of the bar below, with its top extending up above the horizontal bar.

13 Repeat Steps 10 and 11, and remove the extra material to create a perfect miter joint on the left side. Make the Background layer invisible and export to GIF89a (the transparency will be automatically set for you). Name the file "top.gif."

14 Make Layer 2 copy 2 active and choose Layer➡Transform➡Flip Vertical. This will be the first step in creating our bottom frame image. Repeat with the right side image on Layer 2 copy and export the GIF file as "bottom.gif." You may need to move one or both sides up or down a bit to realign them correctly with the horizontal bar.

15 Make Layer 2 active. Make all other layers invisible. Choose the Crop tool and select a section approximately 150 pixels long.

16 After cropping the image, choose Image➡Rotate Canvas➡ 90° CCW. Export to GIF89a, naming it "side.gif."

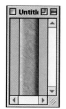

17 Open your HTML editor and create a file with a textured background tile (I used the Maple Tile I used to create the frames). Create a one-row, one-cell table, centered with no border, and place the image "top.gif" into it. Without a return, create a one-row, three-cell table, centered with no border, and place the image "side.gif" in the two outside cells, resizing the cells to the image size. Without a return, create another one-row, one-cell table, centered with no border, and place the image "bottom.gif" into it. You can create a larger frame by "stacking" several images into the middle table's outside cells. The effect looks like one seamless frame.

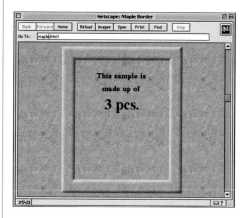

VARIATIONS

For a twist on this effect, you can use virtually any seamless tiled image, and even distort the edges.

Returning to Step 3, open another texture (I used the Split Peas Tile, found in the WebMagic2/Part I/tiles folder on the CD-ROM).

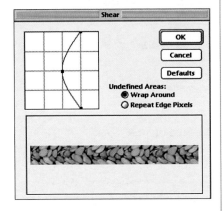

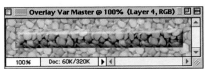

Continue with applying the high-lights and shadows as in Steps 5 through 8, leaving the selection active.

Choose Filter➡Distort➡Shear. Adjust the handles on the line in the graph window until the desired refraction is achieved. Select Wrap Around to keep the edges clean.

Fill a background layer with the same tile pattern at approximately 50% opacity. The final effect looks as if the third bar or frame is made of glass, distorting and enhancing the texture beneath it. ■

PART III

Buttons, Switches, and Arrows

Web navigational graphics are usually superseded by linked text or were made by some HTML "code warrior" resembling something from an early '80s video game. Joining the battle against ugly web sites, you can easily create beautiful, "2 ½-D" (pseudo-3D) buttons and navigational graphics!

Many of the buttons and switches in this section will utilize the textures that can be created in the Backgrounds section. This will give a coordinated and clean look to your finished design.

And, for the more adventurous, many of these buttons and switches can be created with animated up/down sequences that can be controlled with a little Javascript or Shockwave (See Part V, "Tools," for more information). You can even try out samples of working buttons in the WebMagic2/Part III folder on the CD-ROM.

Give the viewer on your web page something to "click on" and keep them there longer!

This is a simple, five-step approach to make a floating, 3D oval button. Its surface is smooth and is perfect for placing text on.

1 Create a new file (128×64, white). Create a new layer (Layer 1). Using the elliptical Marquee tool, draw a horizontal oval selection that fills approximately ⅔ of the image area and fill with a medium foreground color (I chose blue from the Netscape swatch palette).

2 Choose Select➡Modify➡ Contract (five pixels). Choose Select➡Feather (three pixels).

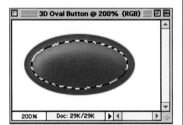

3 Create a new layer (Layer 2). Using the Airbrush tool (Pressure: 11%, 25-pixel soft-edged brush) with the foreground color of white, carefully airbrush the top edge inside the selection. Make sure you concentrate on the 10:00 position of the highlight area to make the effect more believable.

4 Choose Select➡Inverse and make Layer 1 active, making sure that the Preserve Transparency option is set. Set a foreground color that's a darker hue of the base color on the oval. Using the Airbrush tool with the same settings as Step 3, carefully airbrush the bottom 4:00 position. You may hide the selection to make painting easier to see.

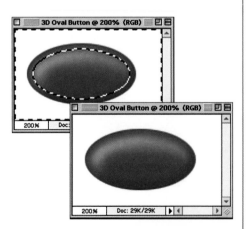

5 Load the transparency selection of Layer 1 and create a new layer just beneath it. Choose Select➡ Feather (three pixels) and fill with the foreground color of black. Deselect the selection and move the shadow layer with the Move tool down and to the right slightly. Adjust the opacity to approximately 50%. There you have it, a 3D button in five easy steps!

VARIATIONS

You can modify the color of this button easily by making Layer 1 active and choosing Image➡ Adjust➡Hue/Saturation➡Colorize (adjust the Hue/Saturation sliders to your desired color effect). ■

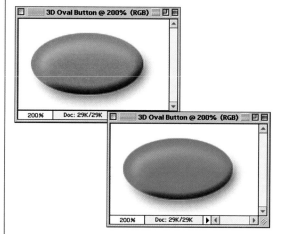

3D arrows are a clean, simple, and effective way to navigate through your web site. They usually look best when shadowed against a white background. It only takes a few steps to create one, and from there the sky's the limit to what you can do to modify them to create dozens more!

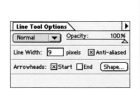

1 Create a new file, (Width: 64 pixels, Height: 32 pixels, White background). Create a new layer (Layer 1). In the Line Tool Options palette (Opacity: 100%, Line Width: nine pixels, Anti-aliased, Arrowheads: Start), click on Shape and set the shape of the arrowheads to a desired proportion. Set the foreground color to black, and draw an arrow from the right side of the image about ³/₄ over to the left side of the image area.

2 Load the transparency selection of Layer 1 and choose Select➡Modify➡Contract (1 pixel). Choose Select➡Feather (1 pixel).

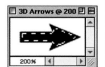

3 Create a new layer above Layer 1 (Layer 2) and set the foreground color to white. Using the Airbrush tool (Pressure: 8%, 9-pixel soft-edged brush), carefully airbrush the top edge inside the selection area to create the illusion of a highlight. Keep in mind that the "light" will be coming in at the 10:00 position, which will make the shadow fall on the 4:00 position. You can hide the selection while painting so you can see what you're doing. (You will always keep this "highlight" layer on top.)

4 Load the transparency selection of Layer 1 and create a new layer just beneath it (Layer 3). Choose Select➡Feather (three pixels) and fill with black. Deselect the selection and using the Move tool, move the shadow down and to the right. Adjust the layer opacity of the layer to approximately 70%. You can repeat this entire process for arrows pointing any direction—just remember to keep your "light" on top, in the 10:00 position, and the "shadow" on the bottom in the 4:00 position.

VARIATIONS

You've only just begun to make 3D arrows. Now that you have the basic components, you can create literally dozens of variations. I'll cover just a few, then you can let your imagination run wild.

Duplicate Layer 1, choose Image➡Adjust➡Hue/Saturation (Saturation: 100, Lightness: 30) and click the Colorize check box. This will turn the black arrow into a bright red. Continue experimenting with this process to achieve several colors. Since you are working with a flat and solid color on that layer, you can also just fill it with a solid color you choose from the Swatches palette. The highlight stays on top, making a reflective highlight on the arrow.

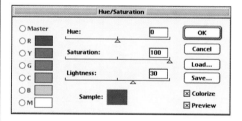

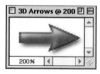

93

Using the preceding process or make the arrow a golden color, to simulate brass.

Next, we'll create a sand arrow from the last step.

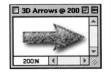

Make sure the Preserve Transparency button is set on the Layers palette on the golden arrow layer. Choose Filter➠Noise➠Add Noise (Amount: 20, Gaussian, Monochromatic).

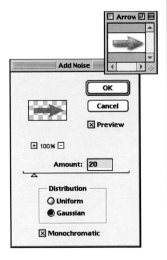

We can continue from the last step to create a wood textured arrow!

Make the Sand layer active and choose Image➠Adjust➠Brightness/Contrast (Contrast: 40).

Choose Filter➠Blur➠Motion Blur (Angle: 10, Distance: 3 pixels). This will give the arrow a nice wood-grain texture.

To make an aluminum texture, just start with the Sand layer again.

Make the Sand layer active, choose Image➡Adjust➡Hue/Saturation (Hue: -90, Saturation: 15), and click the Colorize check box. Choose Image➡Adjust➡Brightness/ Contrast (Contrast: 40). This will set the base color of the aluminum texture. You can add or subtract saturation to your liking.

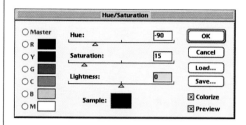

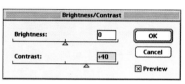

Choose Filter➡Blur➡Motion Blur (Angle: 45, Distance: 8 pixels). You can adjust the angle to your specific needs, but this angle reads the best on this small of an image. Choose Filter➡Sharpen➡Sharpen. This will bring out more of the detail in your brushed aluminum texture.

Just about any texture you want to put inside the arrow selection will work for you. Remember to keep the highlight layer on top and the shadow below. You can control how "shiny" your arrows are by adjusting the opacity of the high-light layer. ■

This dial switch is something you might see on a piece of industrial equipment or an old radio, only with a modern, colorful flair to it. It doesn't take a 3D expert to simulate this effect—just a little practice with the Airbrush tool!

1 Create a new file (64×64, white). Create a new layer (Layer 1). Using the elliptical Marquee tool, draw a circle in the center ⅔ of the image area, and fill with a foreground color (I used a medium blue).

2 Create a new layer (Layer 2). Using the rectangular Marquee tool, draw a vertical box approximately 15 pixels wide from top to bottom of the circle area, being careful not to go outside of the circle.

3 Make Layer 1 invisible. Make Layer 2 active. Fill the selection with the current foreground color. Deselect the selection and choose Layer➡Transform➡Rotate and rotate the rectangle to the left (approximately −30 degrees).

4 Using the Eraser tool (Paintbrush, opacity: 100%, 19-pixel hard-edged brush), click once on the top-right corner of the rectangle, then once again on the top-left corner. This creates a "point" on the end of the rectangle.

5 Select a 27-pixel soft-edged brush and click once on the bottom of the rectangle. This should make the bottom of the "pointer" fade-off. Click again if there's still a hard edge on the bottom. Then use a smaller brush and "fade-in" the indents on the tip of the pointer.

6 Using the Burn tool (Midtones, Exposure: 45, 17-pixel soft-edged brush), apply to the bottom (shadow) edge of the pointer (in this case, the left side only slightly). Choose the Dodge tool (Midtones, Exposure: 45, 15-pixel soft-edged brush), and add "highlights" to the top edges of the pointer.

7 Set the foreground color to white. Using the Line tool (Opacity: 100%, Line Width: 2 pixels, Anti-aliased), draw a line from the tip of the pointer to about halfway down, centered on the shaft.

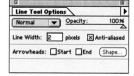

8 Duplicate Layer 2 (Layer 3) and choose Layer➡Transform➡Flip Horizontal. Make Layer 2 invisible.

9 Using the Burn tool (Midtones, Exposure: 45, 17-pixel soft-edged brush), apply to the bottom (shadow) edge of the pointer. Choose the Dodge tool (Midtones, Exposure: 45, 17-pixel soft-edged brush), and add "highlights" to the top edges of the pointer.

10 Make Layer 3 invisible and make Layer 1 active, making sure the Preserve Transparency option is set. Load the transparency selection of Layer 1 and choose Select➡ Modify➡ Contract (three pixels). Choose Select➡Feather (two pixels).

11 Choose Select➡Inverse. Using the Airbrush tool (Pressure: 11%, 17-pixel soft-edged brush) with the foreground color of white, carefully airbrush the top edge (10:00 position) of the circle selection. You may hide the selection to see better what you're painting.

12 Using the Airbrush tool (Pressure: 11%, 17-pixel soft-edged brush) with the foreground color of black, carefully airbrush the bottom shadowed edge (4:00 position) of the circle selection. Deselect the selection when you are finished.

13 Make Layer 2 visible. Duplicate Layer 1. Using the Airbrush tool (Pressure: 11%, 17-pixel soft-edged brush) with the foreground color of black, airbrush a shadow off to the right side of the pointer, just until the right edge of the pointer shows up with a sharp line.

14 Make Layer 3 visible and make Layer 2 invisible. Make Layer 1 active. Using the Airbrush tool (Pressure: 11%, 17-pixel soft-edged brush) with the foreground color of black, airbrush a shadow off to the right side of the pointer, as above, only this time it will be a bit darker.

15 Create a new layer just beneath Layer I and name it Shadow. Using the Airbrush tool (Pressure: 11%, 17-pixel soft-edged brush) with the foreground color of black, carefully airbrush below the bottom shadowed edge (4:00 position) under the dial. Merge the corresponding dial switch layers (left & right), leaving them separate from the shadow for modifying and variations.

VARIATIONS

It's easy to modify the colors of these dial switches with just one step.

Make the switch layer active. Choose Image➟Adjust➟Hue/ Saturation (Colorize) (adjust the hue and saturation to your desired color settings). ■

This shiny, new glass marble effect can be used as a button or a smaller version can be used as bullets. It's a nice 3D effect that you can rotate as an animation as well.

1 Create a new file (64×64, white). Create a new layer (Layer 1) and fill the foreground with red.

2 Set the foreground color to black. Using the Airbrush tool (Pressure: 6%, 9-pixel soft-edged brush), add some diagonal zigzag lines across the red image area.

3 Choose Filter➡Distort➡Glass (Distortion: 10, Smoothness: 5, Texture: Frosted, Scale: 100%). This will give our marble its internal texture.

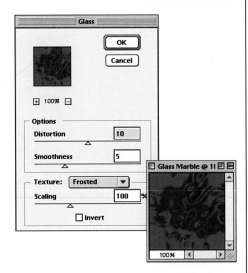

4 Using the elliptical Marquee tool, hold down (Option-Shift)[Alt-Shift] and select an area from the center to about ¾ image area. With the selection active, choose Copy, then Paste. This will create a new layer (Layer 2) from only the selected area. Make Layer 1 and the Background layer invisible.

5 Duplicate Layer 2 (Layer 2 copy). Choose Image➡Adjust➡ Desaturate. Then choose Image➡ Adjust➡Brightness/Contrast (Brightness: 15, Contrast: 85).

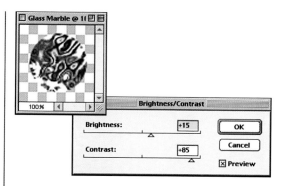

6 Load the transparency selection of Layer 2 copy and copy the selection. Create a new channel and paste. This will be a new selection channel for adjustments.

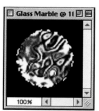

7 Make Layer 2 copy invisible, then duplicate Layer 2 again (Layer 2 copy 2). Load the transparency selection of Channel #4. Then choose Filter➡Artistic➡Plastic Wrap (Highlight: 17, Detail: 12, Smoothness: 3). This will give a "pearlescent" feel to the marble texture.

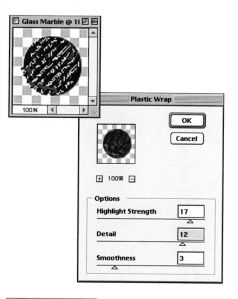

8 Load the transparency selection of Layer 2 copy 2, and create a new layer (Layer 3). Set the foreground color to black. Using the Airbrush tool (Pressure: 6%, 25-pixel soft-edged brush), carefully paint a "shadowed" edge on the 4:00 position of the marble sphere. Set the foreground color to white and

paint a soft highlight area in the 10:00 position on the sphere. Using the polygon Lasso tool, select a 4-sided polygon in the 10:00 position of the sphere to imitate a reflection of an artificial light on the surface. Airbrush white inside this selection. (It's okay if you paint a bit too heavy on this layer, as you can adjust its intensity by adjusting the layer opacity.)

9 Load the transparency selection of Layer 2 and create a new layer (Layer 4) right above the back-ground layer. This will be the shad-ow layer. Choose Select➡Feather (3 pixels). Set the foreground color to black and fill the selection. Deselect the selection and using the Move tool, position the shadow down and to the right of the mar-ble sphere. Adjust the layer opacity (40%). Once you're satisfied with your layer opacity adjustments, merge the visible layers above the shadow layer.

VARIATIONS

It's easy to create different colored marbles once you have the first one completed!

Make the merged marble layer active (not the shadow layer) and choose Image➡Adjust➡Hue/ Saturation (Colorize). We adjusted the Hue slider to several positions to achieve these results.

Hue/Saturation		
○ Master	Hue:	-158	OK
○ R			Cancel
○ Y	Saturation:	79	Load...
○ G			Save...
○ C	Lightness:	0	
○ B	Sample:		☒ Colorize
○ M			☒ Preview

To make your marble appear to "glow" as if it were illuminated from behind, this variation does the trick. (This also makes a great rollover effect.)

Choose Image➟Adjust➟Hue/Saturation (Saturation: 100, Lightness: 15). ■

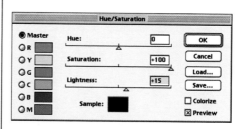

This is a very effective high-tech 3D button with a brushed aluminum texture and a metal bezel around it. It only takes a few steps to create this button from scratch, with no third-party filters or photographic textures!

1 Create a new file (80×40 pixels, white). Create a new layer (Layer 1) and fill with a white foreground color. Choose Filter➡Noise➡Add Noise (Amount: 100, Gaussian, Monochromatic).

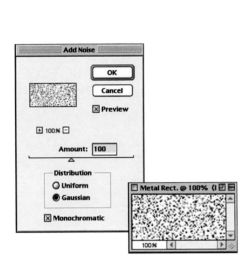

2 Choose Filter➡Blur➡Motion Blur (Angle: 0, Distance: 10 pixels). This will give us the "brushed aluminum" texture.

3 Choose Image➡Adjust➡Hue/Saturation (Colorize) to add a little color to your texture. I used Hue: −120, Saturation: 20, Lightness: −10.

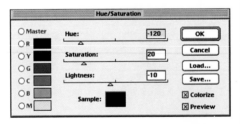

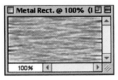

4 Using the rectangular Marquee tool, select an area about five pixels from the edge all around, creating an equidistant border around the selection. Copy and paste the selection. This will create Layer 2. Make Layer 1 invisible.

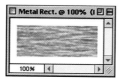

5 Choose the Dodge tool (Highlights, Exposure: 20%, 9-pixel hard-edged brush). Click the upper-left corner of the image on Layer 2. Hold down the Shift key and click the upper-right corner of the image. Repeat until you get the desired "highlight" effect on the top edge, then continue on the left edge of the image.

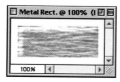

6 Choose the Burn tool (Highlights, Exposure: 20%, 8-pixel hard-edged brush). Click the lower-left corner of the image on Layer 2. Hold down the Shift key and click the lower-right corner of the image. Repeat until you get the desired "shadow" effect on the bottom edge, then continue on the right edge of the image. This alone gives you a nice, clean button to use against any color background.

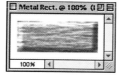

7 Using the Eraser tool (Paintbrush, Opacity: 100%, 8-pixel hard-edged brush), carefully round off the corners of the image on Layer 2. Create a new layer (Layer 3) just beneath Layer 2. Fill the layer with the foreground color of white.

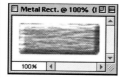

8 Load the transparency selection of Layer 2, and choose Select➡ Modify➡Expand Selection (three pixels). Next, choose Select➡ Modify➡Border (three pixels).

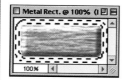

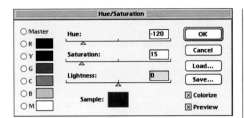

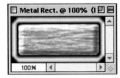

9 Make Layer 3 active and choose Select➡Inverse. Fill the selection with the foreground color of black. Deselect the selection and choose Image➡Adjust➡Hue/Saturation➡ Colorize to give the bezel a metallic coloring. (I used: Hue: –120, Saturation: 15).

VARIATIONS

Just a couple steps makes this a two-part, animated button sequence, with an up and a down!

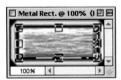

Duplicate Layer 2 (Layer 2 copy). Make Layer 2 invisible and make Layer 2 copy active. Choose Layer➡Transform➡Scale, and click-drag the bounding box in very slightly (only one or two pixels from top and one side). After re-scaling your button, use the Move tool to center it inside the bevel.

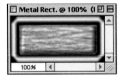

Using the Burn tool, slightly darken the bottom top and right edges of the Layer 2 copy image, giving it a "sunken-in" feeling (you can test your animation by turning Layers 2 copy and 2 on/off alternately to see if they move correctly).

To make your bevel appear to "glow" as if it were neon, try this alternative. (This also makes a great rollover effect!)

Duplicate Layer 3 and name it
"Glow." Choose Image➡Adjust➡
Hue/Saturation➡Colorize
(Saturation: 100, Lightness: 15). ■

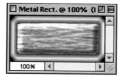

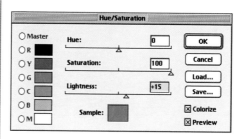

These plastic bars are quick and easy to create, and you can apply several textures to them, making them look just like a 3D model.

1 Create a new file (80×32, white). Choose Select➡All and fill with a foreground color of black. Choose View➡Show Rulers and View➡ Show Guides. Add one horizontal guide centered and add two vertical guides spaced at 15 pixels from each end.

2 Using the Eraser tool (Paintbrush, Opacity: 100%, 25-pixel hard-edged brush), click the intersection of the left guides.

3 Hold down the Shift key and click the intersection of the right guides. Make sure you are centered on the guides when you click, or you will have a crooked button!

4 Choose Select➡All and Copy. Create a new channel and paste.

5 Create a new layer (Layer 1). The transparency selection of Channel #4 should still be active; fill with the foreground color of medium blue (or any color you choose).

Plastic Bars

6 Set the foreground color to white. With the selection still active, use the Airbrush tool (Pressure: 6%, 12-pixel soft-edged brush) to add some soft highlights across the top edge of the selection. Be careful not to paint too much!

7 Set the foreground color to black and carefully airbrush a shadowed area along the bottom edge of the selection.

8 With the selection still active, choose Filter➡Blur➡Motion Blur (Angle: 0, Distance: 10). This will help smooth out any imperfections in the airbrushing and give a nice luster to the surface.

9 Choose Image➡Adjust➡ Brightness/Contrast (Brightness: 20, Contrast: 35). This will bring out the highlights and "plastic" feel of your button.

10 With the selection still active, create a new layer (Layer 2) beneath Layer 1. This will be the shadow layer. Choose Select➡ Feather (two pixels), and fill with the foreground color of black. Deselect the selection and using the Move tool, move the shadow down and to the right. Adjust the opacity of the shadow layer to the desired amount.

VARIATIONS

Applying Textures

Creating different textures on these buttons, using the original as a base is a snap!

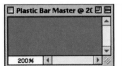

Create a new layer (Layer 2), and fill with a medium color (I chose green). This will be the base to the texture you're creating.

Set the foreground color to black. Using the Airbrush tool (15% Pressure, 5-pixel soft-edged brush), paint some "zebra stripes" at an angle over your solid color.

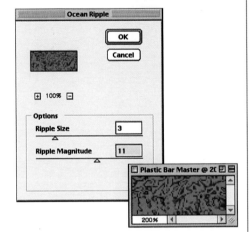

Select Filter➡Distort➡Ocean Ripple (Ripple Size: 3, Ripple Magnitude: 11). This will create a "fractal-like" swirl texture.

Load the transparency selection of Channel #4, choose Select➡Inverse and delete.

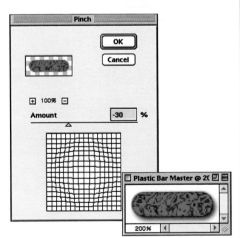

Select Filter➡Distort➡Pinch (Amount: –30). This will give the illusion that the texture is wrapping around the shape of the bar.

Set the Options of Layer 2 to Screen (Opacity: 100%). This will combine the blue with the new texture, revealing the highlights and shadows of the bar shape.

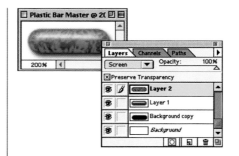

Duplicate Layer 2 (Layer 2 copy), and set the Options of Layer 2 copy to Color (Opacity: 100%). This will keep the shape and high-lights of the bar, but force the color of the new texture.

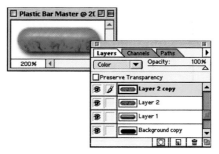

Aliased Edges

If you need to make a button with a transparent background and no drop shadow, then you need to make sure the edges are not anti-aliased. The following steps will help you get a clean, hard edge around your button.

Make only Channel #4 active. Choose Image➟Adjust➟ Brightness/Contrast (Brightness: 25, Contrast: 100). You may need to adjust yours slightly higher or lower until all of the gray pixels disappear.

Make Layer 2 active and load the transparency selection of Channel #4. Choose Selection➟Inverse and delete the selection, using the Delete key. If needed, use the Burn tool lightly around the edges to darken any left over light pixels. Make the Background layer invisible and export to GIF89a. ■

111

Here's a different approach to web page navigation...it's a realistic rocker switch that you might find on a control panel. You can make the up/down sequences and animate them with a JavaScript rollover or use them in a Shockwave movie.

1 Create a new file (32×64, white). Set the foreground color to medium gray. Select➡All and fill with the foreground color.

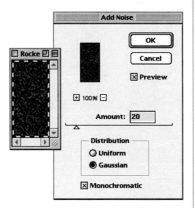

2 Choose Filter➡Noise➡Add Noise (Amount: 20, Gaussian, Monochromatic).

3 Using the rectangular Marquee tool, select an area approximately six pixels inside the image area on all sides. Create a new layer via Copy (Layer 1).

4 Make the Background layer invisible. Make Layer 1 active and select the Dodge tool (Highlights, Exposure: 50%, 7-pixel hard-edged brush). Click once on the upper-left corner of Layer 1. Hold down the Shift key and click once on the top-right corner. Continue back and forth until there is a defined highlighted edge across the top. Repeat down the left side of the image.

5 Choose the Burn tool (Highlights, Exposure: 50%, 7-pixel hard-edged brush). Click once on the lower-left corner of the image on Layer 1. Hold down the Shift key and click once on the lower-right corner of the image. Repeat until you get the desired "shadow" effect on the bottom edge, then continue on the right edge of the image.

6 Duplicate Layer 1 (Layer 1 copy). With the rectangular Marquee tool, select the top half of the image and create a new layer via Cut (Layer 2). This will leave the bottom half of the image on Layer 1 copy.

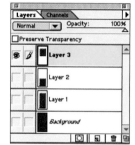

7 Make Layer 1 copy and the Background layer invisible and make Layer 2 active. Using the Burn tool (Midtones, Exposure: 10, 25-pixel soft-edged brush), carefully darken the bottom side of the image on Layer 2. This will create the shadow area of the top half of the switch, creating the illusion that it's protruding from the surface.

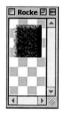

8 Using the Dodge tool with the previously used settings, lighten the top side of the Layer 2 image a bit more, to enhance the effect.

9 Make layer 2 invisible and make Layer 1 copy active. Using the Dodge tool (Highlights, Exposure: 9, 25-pixel soft-edged brush), carefully lighten the top side of the Layer 1 copy image until there is definition between the top/bottom halves of the switch. (Remember to keep the light coming from the 10:00 position, and casting shadows in the 4:00 direction.)

10 Make the Background layer active. Using the Burn tool (Midtones, Pressure: 45, 12-pixel hard-edged brush), gradually work around the perimeter of the switch by clicking once in a corner, holding down the Shift key and moving to the next corner clockwise. This will create a darkened edge around the switch.

11 Duplicate the Background layer (Background copy) and make it active. Using the Airbrush tool (Pressure: 6%, 7-pixel soft-edged brush) with the foreground color of black, airbrush a shadow area around the 4:00 position under the bottom half of the switch. Be careful not to paint too much here.

12 Make Layer 1 copy and the Background copy layer invisible. Make Layer 2 visible. Make the Background layer active. Carefully airbrush the shadow area under the right side of the top half of the switch.

13 Continue "touching-up" edges and shadows by using the Dodge and Burn tools with smaller brush sizes, to enhance the effect of a 3D switch. Merge the "On switch layers" and the "Off switch layers."

VARIATIONS

A nice touch to this switch is to add a power indicator light that glows in the "On" position!

Make the On switch layer visible, and create a new layer (Layer 1). Set the foreground color to a bright red or green. Using the rectangular Marquee tool, select an area centered in the top half of the switch and fill with the foreground color.

Deselect the selection. Using the Airbrush tool (Pressure: 6, 20-pixel soft-edged brush), airbrush a "glowing" area directly over the colored square. This should cause a nice fuzzy glowing effect from the light. (If it looks like you just painted a big blob on it, instead of adding a little glow, then you've gone too far with your airbrushing. Lower your pressure and don't hold it down too long.)

Using the Magic Wand tool (Tolerance: 32, anti-aliased), select the center square of the light area. Make all layers invisible except the Off switch layer. Create a new layer (Layer 2) above the Off switch. Fill the selection with a darker version of the color you used in the On switch light (darker green or red). ■

115

This type effect can make a great "clickable" imagemap area or button! You can apply this technique to banner ads and graphics on your web site as well.

1 Create a new file (128×64, white). Set the foreground color to red. Using the Type tool, place text centered in the image area. This creates Layer 1.

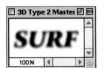

2 Load the transparency selection of Layer 1. Create a new layer just beneath Layer 1 (Layer 2). Choose Select➥Feather (three pixels) and fill with a foreground color of black. Deselect the selection. Make Layer 1 invisible.

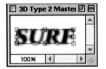

3 Choose Layer➥Transform➥Scale and make the shadow about five pixels smaller in width. Show the Info palette to see the width of the layer as you scale it.

4 Make Layer 1 visible and adjust the layer opacity of Layer 2 to approximately 50%. Using the Move tool, center the shadow under the text.

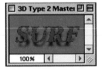

5 Create a new layer just beneath Layer 2 (Layer 3). Fill with a foreground color of a medium aqua from the Swatches palette.

6 Set the foreground color to white. Using the Airbrush tool (Pressure: 11, 13-pixel soft-edged brush), apply a random "webbing" pattern on Layer 3. Adjust the opacity of Layer 3 to lighten the "water." Make all layers visible and merge visible.

7 Choose Filter➡Distort➡Ripple (Amount: 60%, Size: Medium). This makes the type look wavy as if viewing it through water in a pool.

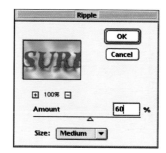

8 Create a new layer (Layer 1). Set the foreground color to dark blue and fill with the foreground color.

9 Using the Paintbrush tool (Pressure: 100%, 100-pixel soft-edged brush) and the foreground color set to white, click twice in the center of the blue layer.

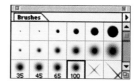

10 Choose Filter➡Distort➡Ocean Ripple (Size: 7, Magnitude: 9).

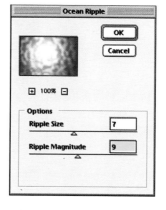

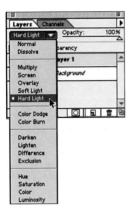

11 Select Hard Light on the Layers palette and adjust the opacity of (Layer 1) to approximately 60%, to create the illusion of water reflecting sky.

12 Create a new layer on top (Layer 2). Fill with black.

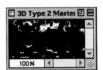

13 Using the Paintbrush tool (Pressure: 100%, 15-pixel soft-edged brush) with the foreground color of white, paint a squiggly line across the top two-thirds of the image area.

14 Choose Filter➠Distort➠Ocean Ripple (Size: 9, Magnitude: 18).

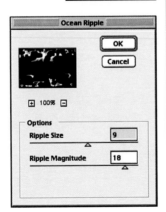

15 Select Lighten on the Layers palette. This will give the illusion of sunlight reflecting on the water. Wanna go for a dip? ■

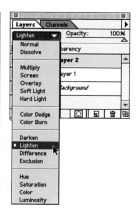

This classic wood button can be created in different sizes and shapes. You can make matching title bars and photo windows using this same technique, for a web page design that shows a lot of class.

1 Create a new file (80×40, white). Create a new layer (Layer 1) and fill the foreground with a medium warm brown from the Swatches palette.

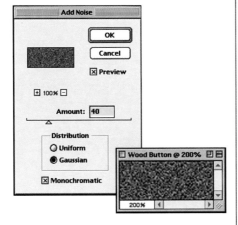

2 Choose Filter➡Noise➡Add Noise (Amount: 40, Gaussian, Monochromatic).

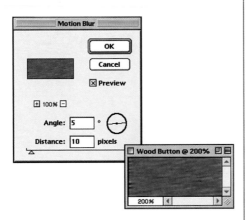

3 Choose Filter➡Blur➡Motion Blur (Angle: 5, Distance: 10). This will give the illusion of a mahogany-like wood grain texture.

4 Using the rectangular Marquee tool, select an area about five pixels from the edge all around, creating an equal-distant border around the selection. Create a new layer via Copy (Layer 2).

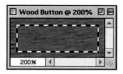

5 Make Layer 1 invisible. Choose the Burn tool (Highlights, Exposure: 20%, eight-pixel hard-edged brush). Click once on the lower-left corner of the image on Layer 2. Hold down the Shift key and click once on the lower-right corner of the image. Repeat until you get the desired "shadow" effect on the bottom edge, then continue on the right edge of the image. This alone gives you a nice, clean button to use against any color background.

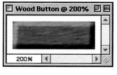
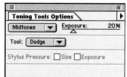

6 Choose the Dodge tool (Highlights, Exposure: 20%, eight-pixel hard-edged brush). Click once on the upper-left corner of the image on Layer 2. Hold down the Shift key and click once on the upper-right corner of the image. Repeat until you get the desired "highlight" effect on the top edge, then continue on the left edge of the image.

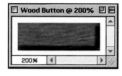
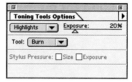

121

7 Using the Eraser tool (Paintbrush, Opacity: 100%, eight-pixel hard-edged brush), carefully round off the corners of the image on Layer 2. Make Layer 1 active. This can be saved as a protruding button as is!

8 Duplicate Layer I (Layer I copy). Load the transparency selection of Layer 2 and choose Select➞Modify ➞Expand Selection (three pixels). Next, choose Select➞Modify➞ Border (three pixels). This will define an area to create a beveled edge around the button.

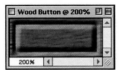

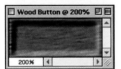

9 Make Layer I copy active. Using the Dodge and Burn tools, add highlights and shadows to the inside of the selection, using the same brush settings as on the button edges. This gives the border around the button a natural, carved bevel edge. You can make Layer 2 invisible for an indented look as well.

VARIATIONS

It's easy to create a "down" button sequence for a two-part Javascript rollover or Shockwave click-down button.

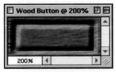

Duplicate Layer 2 (Layer 2 copy). Make Layer 2 invisible and make Layer 2 copy active. Choose Layer➞Transform➞Scale and click-drag the bounding box in very slightly (only one or two pixels from top and one side). After scaling your button, use the Move tool to center it inside the bevel.

To make a matching background texture tile for this button, start by creating a new file (128×128, white). Choose Select➞All and fill with the brown color from Step 1. Repeat Steps 2 and 3, using the same settings.

Choose Filter➡Other➡Offset
(Horizontal: 64). Using the rectangular Marquee tool (Feather: three
pixels), select the center vertical
third of the image area.

Choose Filter➡Blur➡Motion Blur
(Angle: 0, Distance: 6 pixels).
Deselect the selection. This will
smooth out the vertical line running
down the middle of the image.

Choose Filter➡Sharpen➡Unsharp
Mask (Amount: 100%, Radius: 0.3 pixels). This will hide any fuzziness from
the feathered edges. You can test
your background texture by choosing Select➡All then Edit➡Define
Pattern. Create a new file (250×250
pixels, white). Choose Edit➡Fill
(Pattern, 100%, Normal). ■

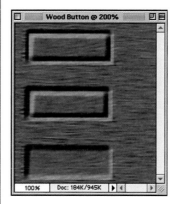

Okay, so you've made some buttons...now, what about labeling them? You don't want to have cheesy type on a cool 3D button you worked so hard to create, do you? Here's a few quick and easy effects for getting your type to really stand out (or sink in)!

1 Open the file called 3D Oval Button on the CD-ROM in the Button Projects folder. It already has the layers created for you.

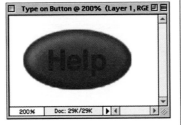

2 Choose a foreground color of a dark blue color. Using the Type tool, insert your text and center the type layer (Layer 2) using the Move tool.

3 Load the transparency selection of Layer 2 and create a new layer just beneath it (Layer 3). Choose Select➡Feather (1 pixel).

124

4 Make Layer 3 active and fill the selection with white. Deselect the selection. Using the Move tool, move Layer 3 down and to the right to create the illusion of a highlighted edge along the inside of the engraved lettering.

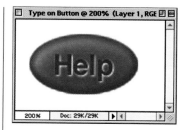

5 Load the transparency selection of Layer 3 and create a new layer just beneath it (Layer 4). Make Layer 4 active, and fill the selection with the dark blue color. Deselect the selection, and using the Move Tool, move Layer 4 up and to the right to create the slightly shadowed, rounded edge of the embossed type. You can adjust the Opacity of the highlight/shadow layers to your desired amount to make the effect more believable.

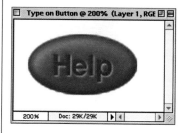

VARIATIONS

To make the type on this button embossed, as if it's protruding from the surface instead of being engraved takes only a couple simple moves. It's just a trick we're playing with light and shadows!

Make Layer 4 active. Using the Move tool, move the layer down into the position that Layer 3 is currently in. This will create the shadow on the other side of the text. Make Layer 3 active, and use the Move tool to place it into the position that Layer 4 was previously. Now that's magic!

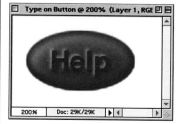

125

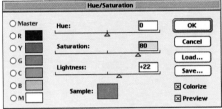

This next variation will give the text the illusion that it's glowing, as if it's lighted from the inside of the button. This makes a great rollover effect.

Duplicate Layer 2, then choose Image➤Adjust➤Hue/Saturation (Colorize, Saturation: 80, Lightness: 22).

You can repeat these effects steps with several buttons made in this section. Here are some examples using the Metal Rectangle and Wood Rectangle buttons:

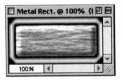

I eliminated the shadow layer on this example because it just made it too muddy.

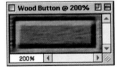

I eliminated the shadow layer on this example, as well.

To give this button a hand-chiseled effect, flatten the file and choose Filter➡Texture➡Texturizer (Sandstone, Scale: 194%, Relief: 2, Light Direction: Top Left). Dig it! ∎

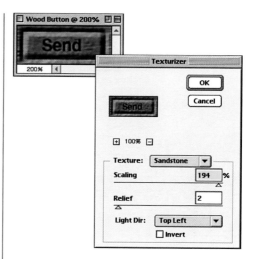

Type on Buttons

Return

Help

PART IV

Animations

Add some pizzazz to your web page designs with entertaining and functional animations. In this section, you will learn how to create animation sequences in Photoshop that are small in size but big in impact.

Sometimes, animations can be made up of a series of only two or three frames, but when looped continuously, appear to be one long animation. When creating any graphics for the Web, especially animations, try to use the same components as many times as possible. They will load once and stay in the browser's cache until called upon again, which will decrease your viewer's load time dramatically.

Many of these animation sequences can be used as navigational graphics as well, simply by creating an animated GIF file, and attaching a link to it. You will learn how to make the animation sequences move in Part V, "Tools." All of these animations can be previewed in the WebMagic2/Part IV folder on the CD-ROM.

Turn the page and get animated! (but don't run with those scissors; you'll poke your eye out!)

Something we've all seen in major corporate sites or search engines are the banner ads, which have to load very quickly, yet get your attention (and hopefully get you to click on them!). They usually have some restrictions on their size (468×60 pixels) and must be in the 216-color palette. The banner here is an example of a banner that has navigational areas as well as eye-catching animation.

1 Create a new file (468×60, white). With the rectangular Marquee tool, drag out an area from the left side of the image to approximately two-thirds of the image area on the right, as shown here. Fill with a medium color (I used bright red).

2a Set the foreground color to a medium blue. Using the Type tool, place a line of text (I chose "Click Here") over the white area of the background; this creates a new layer, Layer 1.

2b Create a new layer (Layer 2) and choose the Line tool (8 Pixels, Arrowhead at start) with the foreground color set to Black. Draw an arrow pointing toward the type below, but keep it clear of running into it.

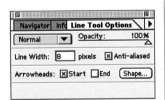

3 Load the transparency selection of Layer 1. Create a new layer (Layer 2) just below Layer 1 and choose Select➡Feather (1 pixel) and fill the selection with black. Deselect the selection and using the Move tool, move the shadow (Layer 2) down and to the right of the type, approximately 3–5 key-strokes with the arrow keys. Set the layer opacity to 50%. This will give the illusion that the type and the arrow are merely "floating" above the background.

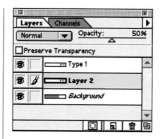

4 Create a new layer (Layer 3). Choose the Polygon Lasso tool and draw a "starburst" on the left side edge of the image area. Fill the selection with yellow as shown, then deselect.

5 Set the foreground to black. Using the Type tool, add some text above the "burst" (I added the word "FREE!"). This will create a new layer (Layer 4). You can rotate or skew the type (Layer 4) into position with the Transform options.

6 Set the foreground color to white. Using the Type tool, type in your first message over the open red space of the image area. Repeat with as many messages as you wish, usually a maximum of four or five so it doesn't take too long to load. Each insertion of text should create a new layer. Make sure to align them with the move tool, positioned directly over one another, so they will make a smooth transition when animated.

Banner Ad Animation

7 While making only one "message" layer visible at a time, export each "message" view with the GIF89a export options, being careful to select 216 Adaptive colors, non-interlaced.

When putting the loop animation together in the GIF animation application, make sure you set the timing of each frame for at least one-second intervals, unless you can easily read the text in less time. You don't want the viewer to miss the message!

You can view this animation in Netscape, by opening the file "bannerad.htm" in the WebMagic2/ Part IV folder on the CD-ROM. You will be able to create your animated GIF, using GIF Builder or GIF Animator, found in the Tools folder on the CD-ROM. ■

Create a real eye-catcher with this bouncing ball on your web page. Using a few paint techniques and motion blur, you can have this realistic 3D ball animation up on your page in minutes.

1 Create a new file (64×240, white). Create a new layer (Layer 1) and set the foreground color to red. Using the elliptical Marquee tool, draw a circle toward the bottom ¼ of the image area. (Holding down (Option-Shift)(Alt-Shift) will make a perfectly round selection from the cursor insertion point.) Fill the selection with red (or another medium-shade color) as shown.

2 Set the foreground color to white. Using the Airbrush tool (10% opacity, 35-pixel soft-edged brush), lightly airbrush an area in the top left side (10:00 position) of the circle to create a highlight area for the sphere. Set the foreground color to black and continue airbrushing a small amount along the bottom-right edge (4:00 position) to create a shadowed area on the sphere as shown.

3 Choose Filter➡Noise➡Add Noise (10, Gaussian, Monochromatic). This will give the ball a bit of texture and make it look a little less "painted" (of course, this step is optional). Deselect the selection.

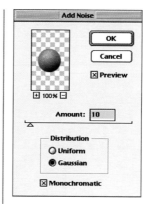

4 Create a new layer (Layer 2) just below the ball layer (Layer 1). Set the foreground color to black. Using the Airbrush tool (10% Opacity, 35-pixel soft-edged brush), airbrush a soft shadow just under the ball as shown. Make sure to make it fairly dark so that you can adjust the layer opacity later.

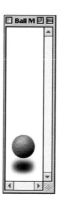

5 Duplicate Layer 1 (Layer 1 copy). Make Layer 1 invisible and make Layer 1 copy active. Choose Layer➡Transform➡Numeric. (Scale, Width: 90%, Height: 110%). This will slightly "squish" the ball on Layer 1 copy.

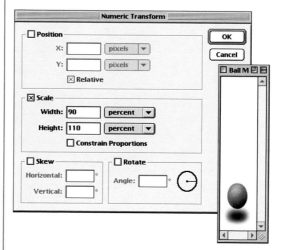

135

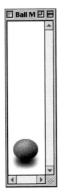

Bouncing Ball

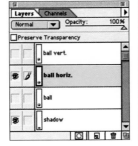

6 Make Layer I copy invisible. Duplicate Layer I (Layer I copy 2) and make Layer I invisible again. Repeat Step 5 on Layer I copy 2, setting the scale to Width: 100% and Height: 90%. This will "squish" the ball on Layer I copy 2 the other direction.

7 Make Layer I copy 2 invisible. Duplicate Layer I copy (Layer I copy 3). Choose Filter➡Blur➡ Motion Blur (Angle: 90, Distance: 15 pixels). This will create the effect that the ball is in vertical motion.

136

8 Create a new layer (Layer 3) on top. Using the rectangular Marquee tool, select an area of the top ⅓ of the image area. Double-click the Marquee tool and set the feather to 10 pixels. By holding down the (Option)[Alt] key, click-drag de-select from the bottom of the selection about ½ way up the selection as shown. Fill the selection with white. This will give the animation a sense that the ball is just disappearing off the page, instead of a hard, abrupt cut-off at the top.

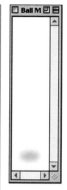

9 Make all layers invisible except for Background, Layer 2, and Layer 3. Adjust the opacity of the shadow (Layer 1 copy) to approximately 25%. Export this as frame 01, using the GIF89a export option from the File menu.

Make Layer 1 copy 3 active. Using the Move tool, move the ball up toward the top of the image area, just beneath the fade-out on Layer 3, as shown. (Holding down Shift while dragging the image locks it horizontally.) Export this as frame 02.

10 Continue this process two more times, moving the blurred vertical ball layer down in equal distance, and adjusting the opacity of the shadow (Layer 2) by 10% increments. Export as frames 03 and 04 accordingly.

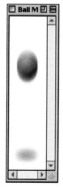

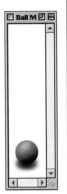

11 Repeat this process once more, moving Layer 1 copy 3 down in equal distance, and adjusting the opacity of the shadow (Layer 2) by 10%. Make Layer 1 copy active and move it with the Move tool, just below the top edge of the blurred layer image. Export as frame 05.

12 Make Layer 1 copy and Layer1 copy 3 invisible and make Layer 1 active. Using the Move tool, move it into position toward the bottom of the image area, resting on the shadow. Adjust Layer 2's opacity to about 60% (or darkest setting you prefer). Export as frame 06.

13 Make Layer 1 invisible and make Layer 1 copy 2 active. Move it into position with the Move tool selected and using the arrow keys, about two pixels below where the last ball rested. This will give the illusion that the ball is compressed against the "floor." Export as frame 07.

14 Make Layer 1 copy 2 invisible and make Layer 1 copy visible. Make Layer 1 copy 3 active and using the Move tool, center the blurred ball directly over the ball on Layer 1 copy below. Export as frame 07.

When putting this animation sequence together in the GIF animation application, duplicate and use the first three frames you created as the last three frames, in reverse order. This will create a loop that appears to bounce forever. You can view the finished GIF animation in Netscape, with the file named bounce.html in the Web-Magic2/Part IV folder on the CD-ROM. ■

This effect is similar to the reader boards you see in a cafe or a bus station, where the words scroll across giving you an advertisement or news headlines. This is sometimes done by a JavaScript, but in that case it relies on the font that the viewer's browser is set to, not necessarily what you want them to see. This effect uses whatever font you want to display, and it can, of course, be as long, or short, as you'd like to make it.

1 Create a new file (320×16, black). Set the foreground color to a light contrasting color (I chose an orange-gold color). Using the Type tool, enter the text in the middle of the image, centering it with the Move tool if necessary. This will create a new layer (Layer 1). (This may take some experimenting with the spacing amount to get it to run all the way across your image area, as shown.) Export as frame 01 using the GIF89a export option.

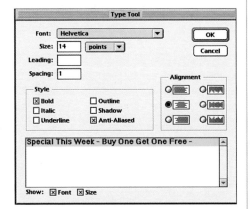

2 Duplicate Layer 1 (Layer 2). Make sure the Preserve Transparency box is unchecked on Layer 2. Choose Filter➡Blur➡Blur More. Then choose Image➡Adjust➡Brightness/Contrast (Brightness: 15, Contrast: -5). This will give the appearance of glowing type that you can flash while the text is in the stationary position in the animation. Export this as frame 02.

3 Make Layer 2 invisible and make Layer 1 active. Choose Filter➡ Other➡Offset (Horizontal: 32, Vertical: 0, Wrap Around). This will "push" the text around to the other end of the image window. Export as frame 03. Repeat several times until you reach the point that you started, creating a continuous loop.

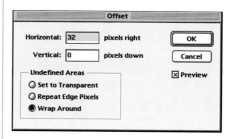

TIP **It is important to make sure the number you offset horizontally is directly divisible into the width of your image area or you won't end up back in the same place you started! (I chose 32, which will give me 10 frames of animation in my 320 pixel-wide image).**

When putting this animation together in a GIF animation application, make sure that the animation stops on the first frame and alternates between the first and second frames a few times to give the effect that the words are pausing and flashing. This also gets the viewer's attention and makes it easier to read the entire message all at once onscreen.

You can see the finished animation using Netscape and opening the file "chasing.html" in the Web-Magic2/Part IV folder on the CD-ROM. ▪

141

142

Ever see one of those television commercials with type that jumps around onscreen? It really gets your attention and is easier to create than you might think. Here are a couple of examples that work with only three frames and load fast; they're only 11K in size!

1 Create a new file (240×64, white). Set the foreground color to a dark color and insert some text with the Type tool. This creates a new layer (Layer 1). Center your text in the middle of the image area, using the Move tool.

2 Adjust the opacity of Layer 1 to 30%. Create an individual layer for each letter by choosing the Type tool and typing over the original type layer, one letter at a time. (Remember, Photoshop 4.0 generates a new layer each time you insert a letter, naming them consecutively, Layer 2, Layer 3, and so on.) You will have a new layer for every letter in your text message.

3 Making one layer at a time active, you can rotate, distort, or skew each letter slightly from the original position. Choose from: Layer➡Transform➡Rotate (or Skew, Scale, Distort).

4 Once you have changed each letter from its original position, hide
the original layers and export as
frame 01 using the GIF89a export
option in the File menu. Duplicate
each text layer once more and hide
the layers from the first set of distortions. Apply the distortions
again, only in a slightly different
direction from the first application,
as shown. Export as frame 02.
Repeat again and export as frame
03. You should have 3 frames with
different versions of the distortions
for each letter. (This may create a
lot of layers if your message is
lengthy.)

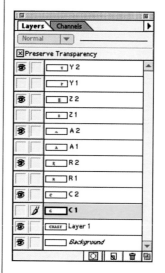

5 By combining the three distorted
versions of the type with the original type layer, you'll be able to put
them together in a GIF animation
application and set them to loop in
a fast, "dancing" fashion.

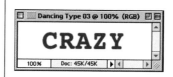

143

VARIATIONS

This variation of dancing type is really easy, yet very effective in getting one's attention in a more subtle way. It appears that the letters are slightly "shaken" like they're in an earthquake.

Repeat Steps 1 and 2 above, but instead of distorting the text in Step 3, move each letter slightly out of registration with the original layer, as shown.

Repeat this process two more times, being careful not to make your adjustments too drastic or forgetting to move a letter. This may lessen the final effect. Export each variation as a GIF89a file and assemble as a loop with a GIF animation application.

To make these letters really pop off the page, you can apply a drop shadow behind them.

Make the first set of distorted letters visible and hide the second and third sets. Merge the visible layers and choose Layer➥Duplicate Layer, then choose New from the Document pop-up menu in the Duplicate Layer dialog box. This creates a new document containing one layer (Layer 1) that shows the first set of distorted letters. Do the same for the second and third layers.

Open one of the newly created files and create a new layer (Layer 2) just under the type layer (Layer 1). Load the transparency selection of Layer 1. Choose Selection➡ Feather (2 pixels).

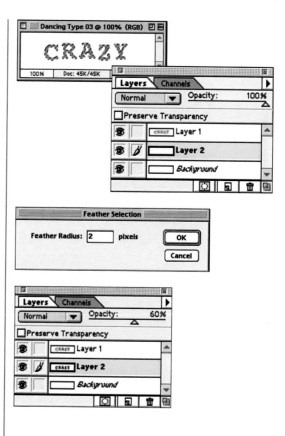

Fill the selection with black and deselect the selection. Using the Move tool, move the shadow (Layer 2) just down and to the left of the type. Adjust the opacity of Layer 2 to approximately 60%.

Repeat this process with the other two variation files and export each with the GIF89a export option. Put them together in the GIF animation application and set them to run about 5 to 10-hundreths of a second. This will create the illusion of type "dancing" above the page.

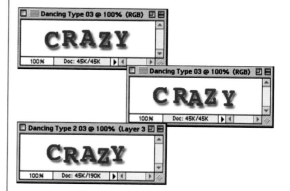

145

You can view the animation samples with Netscape Navigator or Internet Explorer, by opening the file "dance.html" in the Web-Magic2/Part IV folder on the CD-ROM. ■

Here's a great way to add a clean, animated title or message that seems to jump out of nowhere. It looks like embossed letters pushing up out of the background. "Hey! Where did that come from?"

1 Create a new file, (360×64, white). Export a copy of this all-white image as frame 01 of the animation effect using the GIF89a export function. Set the foreground color to black. Enter the text using the Type tool and center your text (Layer 1) in the middle of the image area with the Move tool.

2 Load the selection of Layer 1. Create a new layer (Layer 2) just below Layer 1. With the selection still active, choose Select➡Feather (three pixels), then fill the selection with black. This will be the shadow layer.

3 Load the selection of Layer 1. Create a new layer (Layer 3) just above Layer 1. With the selection still active, choose Select➡Feather (1 pixel), then fill the selection with white. This will be the highlight layer.

4 Deselect and make Layer 1 invisible. Make Layer 2 active and adjust the opacity of the layer to 10%. Export as frame 02 with the GIF89a export option.

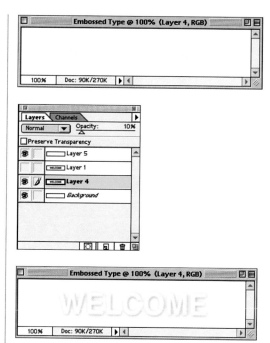

5 Adjust the opacity of Layer 2 to 20%, and export as frame 03 of the animation. Choose the Move tool, and using the arrow keys on your keyboard, click once on the down arrow and once on the right arrow. Adjust the opacity of Layer 2 to 30% and export as frame 04.

6 Repeat this process, moving the arrow keys one click at a time, and increasing the opacity of Layer 2, 10% each step to a maximum of six steps (60% opacity). You should have six frames in this sequence (not including the blank white background frame).

7 Put these sequences together in the GIF animation application and loop them to go backward then forward in sequential order. This will create the illusion of the text being pushed through the back side of the paper.

This animation sample can be viewed with Netscape Navigator or Microsoft Exploder, by opening the file "embossed.html" in the Web-Magic2/Part IV folder on the CD-ROM. ■

One way to get your viewer's attention with an animation is to leave the type stationary, but flash background images behind it. This effect is used in television commercials a lot, but is fairly unique to the web!

1 Create a new file (240×32, white). Set the foreground color to a medium color (I used a golden-yellow color). Enter text using the Type tool and center your text layer (Layer 1) in the middle of the image area.

2 Load the transparency selection of Layer 1. Create a new layer (Layer 2) just below the type layer, and choose Select➡Feather (1 pixel).

3 Fill the selection with black and deselect. Using the Move tool, move the shadow (Layer 2) down and to the right of the type. Adjust the layer opacity of the shadow to 50% and choose Darken mode.

4 Make Layer 1 active. Using the Dodge tool (Midtones, 25%, 13-pixel soft-edged brush), lightly brush the top edges of the type, to give them a bit of highlight for dimension and to make the text stand out more when against mid-toned backgrounds.

5 Open a photo tile from the Web-Magic2/Part I/tiles folder on the CD-ROM (I chose "Chocolate Chips" for this image). You can use other tiles you've created, or photos and scans of any kind. Choose Select➡All and then Edit➡Define Pattern. Activate the Background layer of your project file, choose Select➡All then Edit➡Fill (Pattern, Opacity: 100%, Normal).

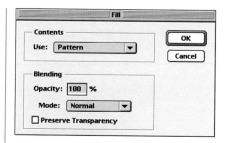

6 Export this frame using the GIF89a export option in the File menu (Adaptive palette, 216 colors, non-interlaced).

151

7 Repeat this process of filling the background layer with assorted photos and textures, exporting each frame as you go (I've used all photos from the tiles folder on the CD-ROM). When putting the frames together in a GIF animation application, be sure to set the timing of the loop fast enough to scroll through the images quickly, but make sure the images "register" to the eye (usually about $^{25}/_{100}$ of a second or more).

You can view this animation with Netscape, by opening the file "flashing.html" in the WebMagic2/Part IV folder on the CD ROM.

VARIATIONS

For the most effective results, choose photos and graphics that work into the "theme" of your web page (such as car photos for an automobile-related web page; building materials for a contractor's site, and so on).

This animation sample can be viewed with Netscape Navigator or Microsoft Explorer, by opening the file "embossed.html" in the WebMagic2/Part IV folder on the CD-ROM. ■

Navigational tools and buttons sometimes get lost on a web page, but these flying arrows will be sure to get their attention! When linked as a graphic in the HTML editor, they will serve as a moving button. The arrow appears to be "hovering" in a defined area, just waiting to be clicked. (Try to catch the arrow and click it!)

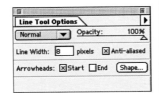

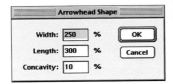

1 Create a new file (64×64, white). Create a new layer (Layer 1). Set the foreground color to black and choose the Line tool (8 pixels, Anti-aliased, Arrowhead at Start, Width: 250%, Length: 300%, Concavity: 10%), draw a right-pointing arrow in the center of your image area.

2 Load the transparency selection of Layer 1. Create a new layer (Layer 2), just below the arrow layer, and choose Select➡Feather (three pixels).

3 Fill the selection with black and deselect. Using the Move tool, move the shadow (Layer 2) down and to the right of the type.

4 Load the transparency selection of Layer 1 and make Layer 1 active. Choose Select➡Modify➡Contract (1 pixel), then choose Select➡ Feather (one pixel).

5 Set the foreground color to white. Using the Airbrush tool (8% opacity, 9-pixel soft-edged brush) and brush along the top edge to create a 3D effect on the arrow as shown.

6 Choose Select➡Inverse. Set the foreground color to black. Make sure Preserve Transparency is on for Layer 1. Using the Airbrush Tool (8% Opacity, 10-pixel soft-edged brush), brush along the bottom edge of the arrow to create a 3D shadow effect.

7 Make Layer 2 active and set the layer opacity to 60%. Export this frame in the GIF89a export option.

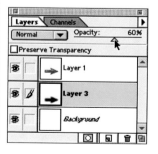

8 Using the Move tool, slightly move the arrow toward the top of the image area. Adjust the opacity of the shadow (Layer 2) to approximately 5–10% less. Export the frame.

9 Repeat the process, moving the arrow around, and matching the shadow in position and adjusting the opacity of the shadow layer. Export frames accordingly.

This animation sample can be viewed with Netscape Navigator or Microsoft Explorer, by opening the file "embossed.html" in the WebMagic2/Part IV folder on the CD-ROM. ■

Flying Arrows

Remember the television show *Knight Rider*? (I'm referring to the car, not the "lifeguard.") These glowing rods that move across the page will remind your viewer of the sequencing lights on the front of the famous talking car.

1 Create a new file (500×16, white). Create a new layer (Layer 1) and fill with black. Choose Show Rulers and Show Guides. Place a horizontal guide centered vertically in the image area. Place a vertical guide 15 pixels from the left edge and another approximately 70 pixels from the left edge. Using the Eraser tool (100%, Paintbrush, 9-pixel hard-edged brush), click once on the left guide intersection. Hold down the Shift key and click once on the right guide intersection. This will create an oblong "window" in the black layer.

2 Using the rectangular Marquee tool, drag out an area from the left edge to an equal distance to the right side of the "window" opening. Choose Select→Inverse and delete the contents of the selection. This will eliminate all of the black on the layer except for the "frame" around the window we created. Load the selection of Layer 1 and duplicate the window frame by choosing the Move tool and, holding down (Option)[Alt], drag the selection to the right, as shown here. (Holding down the Shift key will lock the selection vertically while placing it.)

3 Repeat this process until you've filled the entire layer across the image area (approximately five "windows").

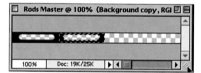

4 Make the Background layer active and fill with a medium color (I chose a golden-yellow color).

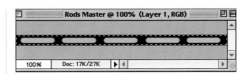

5 Create a new layer (Layer 2), and place beneath Layer 1. Choose the Airbrush tool (10% opacity, 10-pixel soft-edged brush) and set the foreground color to black. Click once on the lower-left side of the image area. Hold down the Shift key and click once on the lower-right side of the image area. Repeat this process until there appears to be a soft, shadowed edge to the bottom of the bar windows. Set the foreground color to white and repeat the process on the upper edge of the image area, until desired effect is achieved. Choose Filter➡Blur➡ Gaussian Blur (.5 pixels) to smooth out the color for a "matte" finish.

6 Choose Image➡Adjust➡ Hue/Saturation to add a richness to the color and to darken it slightly. (I used Saturation: 100, Lightness: −40).

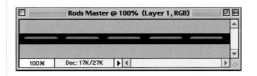

159

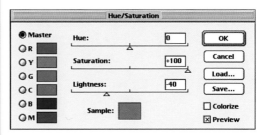

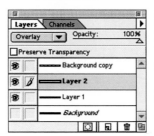

7 Create a new layer (Layer 3) just above the background layer. Set the layer's blending mode to Overlay. Using the Airbrush tool (10% opacity, 10-pixel soft-edged brush) set the foreground color to a lighter version of the background color (I used a lighter yellow color), paint inside one of the small "windows" until it's lightened to the desired level to indicate that this light is "on."

8 To get an even brighter effect, create a new layer (Layer 4) just below Layer 1 (blending layer mode: Normal) and paint with the foreground color set to white with the Airbrush tool over the top of the lightened area you just created, until the desired effect is reached. Then merge the two lightened layers. Using the Move tool, move the lightened layer to the first window and export the frame in the GIF89a file format. Repeat and export a frame for each window position across the image. This animation will go from left to right, giving the illusion that the lights "chase" across the screen. You can choose to reverse the order in the GIF animation application to make the lights chase both directions.

You can view this sample animation in Netscape Navigator or Microsoft Explorer, by opening the file "glowrods.html" in the WebMagic2/ Part IV folder on the CD-ROM.

VARIATIONS

You can customize your finished glowing rods by matching the background texture to that of your web page quite easily!

Make Layer I active and select all. Fill selection with a matching solid color to your background on your web page. Export frames accordingly.

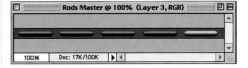

Open the background tile texture file you are using for your web page (I used the Embossed MicroGrid tile found in the WebMagic2/Part I folder on the CD-ROM). Choose Select➡All then Edit➡Define Pattern. Return to your glowing rods file and make Layer I active and Select All. Fill selection (Pattern, 100%, Normal). Export frames accordingly. ◼

Need glasses? Your viewers may think they do when they see this effect! This is a clever way to draw attention with text that starts out-of-focus and transforms into a sharp, readable image.

1 Create a new file, (128×128, white) although you may choose to use a colored background, as I did in this example. Set the foreground color to red. Insert text using the Type tool, and center your text (Layer 1) in the middle of the image area with the Move tool.

2 Load the selection Layer 1 and create a new layer (Layer 2), just under Layer 1. Choose Select➡ Feather (two pixels).

3 Make Layer 2 active and fill the selection with black to create a shadow. Deselect the selection. Using the Move tool, move the shadow (Layer 2) down and to the right. Set the layer opacity to 50%. This will dither the effect instead of creating large, lumpy-looking edges. Flatten the image and export as frame 01, using the GIF89a export option in the File menu (System Palette, 216 colors, Use Best Match).

4 Choose Filter➥Blur➥Radial Blur (Amount:15, Spin, Best). Export as frame 02.

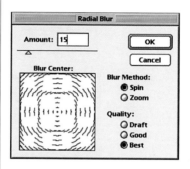

5 Repeat the filter by using (Command-F)[Control-F] on the keyboard, up to about six times; being sure to export and name each frame after each application of the filter. When putting the animation together in the GIF animation application, you may choose to duplicate the sequence forward and backward to make a continuous loop.

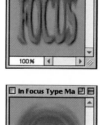

You can view this animation in Netscape by opening the file "focus.html" in the WebMagic2/Part IV folder on the CD-ROM.

VARIATIONS

You may choose to just have the text come into focus without rotating. Starting with Step 4 above:

Choose Filter➥Blur➥Gaussian Blur (two pixels). Export the frame accordingly.

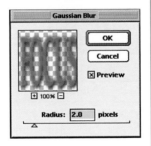

Repeat this process five or six times until you reach your desired effect. ■

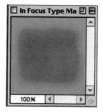

Here's a series of effects for creating rollover sequences for your JavaScript or Shockwave buttons. You can get more information on JavaScripts and Shockwave in the "Tools" section of the book.

1 Create a new file (32×32, white). Create a new layer (Layer 1). Using the rectangular Marquee tool, draw out a square area slightly larger than half of the image area and fill the selection with white. Using the Airbrush tool (10%, 9-pixel soft-edged brush), and the foreground color set to a medium gray, brush diagonal strokes across the selection.

2 Choose Select➡Modify➡ Contract (4 pixels). Create a new layer (Layer 2) and fill the selection with a medium color (I chose green).

3 With the Preserve Transparency option turned on for Layer 2, choose the Dodge tool (Highlights, Exposure: 25%, 5-pixel hard-edged brush) and click on the upper-left corner of the green square. Hold down the Shift key and click on the upper-right corner of the green square. Repeat on the left side of the green square. Choose the Burn tool (Highlights, Exposure: 25%, 5-pixel hard-edged brush) and apply similarly to the bottom and right side edges of the green square. This will create a soft, natural beveled edge.

4 Choose Filter➡Artistic➡Plastic Wrap (Highlight Strength: 12, Detail: 15, Smoothness: 3). This will give the square a plastic-like, 3D texture.

Plastic Wrap

OK

Cancel

100%

Options
Highlight Strength 12
Detail 15
Smoothness 3

5 Duplicate Layer 2 (Layer 2 copy) and choose Image➡Adjust➡ Brightness/Contrast (Brightness: −10, Contrast: 30). Export the image as the "On" button, using the GIF89a or JPEG (.JPG) file formats. Make Layer 2 copy invisible and export as the "Off" button.

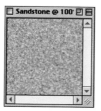

VARIATIONS

You can use any background texture you like with this button sequence to work it into the design of your web page.

Open the background tile texture file you are using for your web page (I used the Sandstone tile found in the WebMagic2/Part I folder on the CD-ROM). Choose Select➡All then Edit➡ Define Pattern. Return to your button file and make the Background layer active. Fill the selection with the pattern (100%, Normal).

167

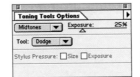

Make the Background layer active and choose the Dodge/Burn tools. Apply the Burn tool to the area above and to the left of the green button, to create a concave, sunken look. Apply the Dodge tool to the areas below and to the right of the green button to highlight the edges of the indention. Export the frames accordingly.

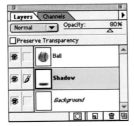

Load the transparency selection of Layer 1 and choose Select➡ Inverse. Choose Select➡Feather (one pixel) and delete. This will give a nice soft edge from the green button to the sandstone indentation.

Another easy rollover effect is to just modify an existing photo.

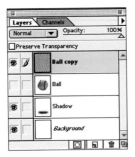

Open an image in the Stock Folder on the CD-ROM. Create a new layer (Layer 2) under the ball layer. Using the Airbrush tool (10% opacity, 15-pixel soft-edged brush) and the foreground color set to black, carefully brush in a drop shadow directly under the ball. Export the frame accordingly.

Duplicate the ball layer and choose Layer➡Transform➡Rotate. Slightly rotate the ball to the left or right. Export the frame accordingly. This makes a good animated GIF loop file, too!

You can try this rollover sample in the WebMagic2/Part IV folder on the CD-ROM. ■

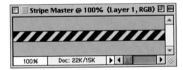

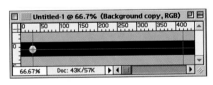

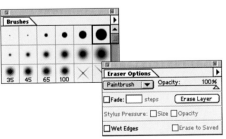

This animation gives the illusion that a three-dimensional bar is rotating clockwise across the page, but in reality it's only two frames of animation that load almost instantly.

1 Create a new file (500×26, black). Create a new layer (Layer 1) and set the foreground color to yellow. Using the Line Tool (10–12 pixels, anti-aliased), draw a single line from bottom to top at a 45 degree angle. Repeat with another line approximately a line-width to the right as shown here.

2 Using the rectangular Marquee tool, select the two diagonal lines and duplicate them by choosing the Move Tool and holding down (Option)[Alt], and dragging the selection to the right, equal in distance of the space between the lines. Make sure you hold down Shift when you move the selection to lock it into position vertically.

3 Repeat this process several times, until you've filled the entire width of the image area with the diagonal striped lines on one layer, as shown here. Flatten the image and save, but keep the file open.

4 Create a new file (500×32, transparent). Create a new layer (Layer 2), choose Select➡All and fill the selection with black. Choose Show Rulers and Show Guides. Place a horizontal guide centered vertically down the image area. Place two vertical guides, just 30 pixels in from each edge. Choose the Eraser tool, (Paintbrush, 100% opacity) and select a 19-pixel hard-edged brush. Click on the intersection of the guides on the left.

5 Hold down the Shift key and click on the intersection of the guides on the right. This will create a long window with rounded ends in the top black layer as shown. Hide Rulers and Guides.

6 Returning to the stripe file, choose Select➡All and copy to the clipboard. On the new file with the window, make Layer 1 active, and paste the clipboard image onto Layer 1.

7 Create a new layer (Layer 3), located above the stripe (Layer 1) and below the window (Layer 2). Choose the Airbrush tool (8% opacity, 9-pixel soft-edged brush), and set the foreground color to black. Click once on the bottom left edge of the new layer. Hold down the Shift key and click once on the bottom right of the layer. Repeat this process back and forth until a nice "shadowed" dark edge appears along the under-side of the striped "bar" as shown here.

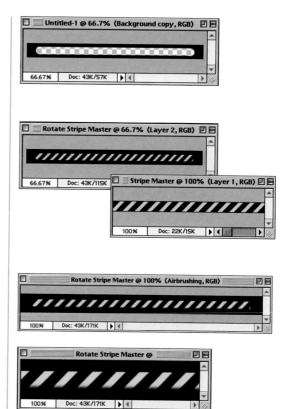

171

8 Set the foreground color to white, and click once at the top left edge of the image. Hold down the Shift key and click on the upper-right edge. Repeat this process back and forth until there is a soft "light reflection" on the top side of the "bar." Touch up the ends of the window with the Airbrush Tool as necessary. This will enhance the 3D effect of the bar and make it appear as though it's in a glass tube.

9 Duplicate Layer 1 (Layer 1 copy) and set the layer opacity to 50%. Using the Move tool, move the layer to the right (while holding down the Shift key, to keep it locked in the vertical position) until the stripes line up in between the stripes of the layer beneath it.

Set the layer opacity of Layer 1 copy back to 100% and export the image using the GIF89a export option. Make Layer 4 invisible and export the second image. When putting the animation together in a GIF animation application, make sure to adjust the speed of the loop (approximately 5–7/100 of a second) so the animation runs smoothly, but not too fast or jumpy.

You can view this animation in Netscape, by opening up the file "stripes.html" in the WebMagic2/Part IV folder on the CD-ROM. ■

174

Like the Microtiles effect, this little animation really loads fast and can be added all over a page without bogging-down the browser. It has only three frames of animation, but when looped, you'd swear it had more. This effect does require some basic drawing skills and copying, but with a little practice, you'll be up and running in no time!

1 Create a new file, (32×32, white). Create a new layer (Layer 1) and zoom in to 300%. Set the foreground color to black. Using the Line tool (one pixel, Anti-aliasing: Off), create a box with four lines, leaving off the corners, so it will appear to be round when we zoom out later. Next, draw a straight line from the center of the bottom of the box to just below the halfway point of the image area, as shown.

2 Adjust the opacity of Layer 1 to 70%. Create a new layer (Layer 2). Using the Line tool, draw arms and legs in motion, as shown here. After drawing this, Adjust the opacity of Layer 2 to 50%. This way you'll be able to see through it when drawing on your next layer.

3 Create a new layer (Layer 3), then draw with the Line tool, making the arms and legs go back about halfway, as shown here. After drawing this, Make Layers 1 and 2 invisible and adjust the opacity of Layer 3 to 50%.

4 Create a new layer (Layer 4) and draw in the next arm and leg sequence as shown. Notice how the legs start to return and cross over here.

5 Return all layer opacity settings to 100%, and make Layers 3 and 4 invisible. Export this image as frame 1 in the GIF89a file format. Make Layer 1 invisible and make Layer 2 visible. Export this image as frame 2. Make Layer 2 invisible and make Layer 3 visible. Export this image as frame 3.

When putting these frames together in a GIF animation application, be sure to set the timing to approximately $^{10}/_{100}$ of a second and loop the animation.

To give this animation a more fluid running pattern, slightly adjust the frames in the GIF animation application. Start with the first frame, move it slightly upward, and then the next frame about half as much. Leave the third frame alone and then duplicate the second frame (which has already been moved slightly upward from it's original position), so you will have a smooth running loop, only four frames long!

VARIATIONS

This variation applies a simple emboss to it.

Flatten each frame (without saving) and choose Filter➡Stylize➡Emboss (1 pixel, Angle: -135). Export frame with the GIF89a file format. Choose File➡Revert after you've exported each frame.

Repeat this process for the other two frames and export. Continue with the GIF animation application.

You can view this animation sample with Netscape Navigator or Microsoft Explorer, by opening the file running.html in the WebMagic2/Part IV folder on the CD-ROM. ■

Text pop-ups are quite helpful in keeping a clean web page design. They're really quite simple to produce and a simple JavaScript or Shockwave file can make them appear "instantly" with a rollover of the cursor. You can get more information on JavaScripts and Shockwave in the Part V, "Tools."

1 Create a new file (128×64, white). Create a new layer (Layer 1). Using the elliptical Marquee tool, draw out an area about ⅓ of the width from the left edge and fill the selection with medium blue.

2 Create a new layer (Layer 2), just above Layer 1 and choose Select➡ Modify➡Contract Selection (two pixels). Then choose Select➡ Feather (one pixel).

3 Set the foreground color to white and double-click the Airbrush tool. Set the opacity to 8% and select the 27-pixel soft-edged brush. Lightly paint across the top area inside the selection on the top layer (be sure to keep the selection active). This will give this "button" a soft, highlighted edge, creating a 3D illusion.

4 Choose Select➡Inverse and make Layer 1 active. Be sure to turn on preserve transparency. Set the foreground color to black and carefully airbrush along the bottom edge of the oval. This will give the object a shadowed edge, enforcing the 3D effect.

5 Merge Layers 1 & 2 and save the file in the Photoshop format. Load the selection Layer 1 (the now-merged layer) and create a new layer (Layer 2) right below it. Choose Select➡Feather (three pixels) and fill the selection with black, creating a shadow. Deselect the selection. Using the Move tool, move the shadow (Layer 2) down and to the right of the oval. Adjust the layer opacity to 60%.

6 Duplicate Layer 1 (Layer 1 copy). Choose Image➡Adjust ➡Hue/Saturation. Click on Colorize (Hue: 0, Saturation: 100, Lightness: 0). This will change the color of the new oval to red.

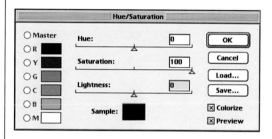

7 Repeat the duplication and colorization process, adjusting the hue in each new button layer to create a different color. Make as many buttons as you need for the text pop-ups. Choose Show Rulers and Show Guides, and add a vertical guide approximately half of the distance across as shown here.

8 Enter text using the Type tool. With the Move tool, place your text centered vertically against the right side of the guide as shown here. Repeat this process on different layers for the number of buttons you've created.

177

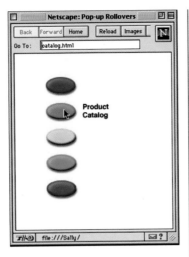

9 Export each button with and without its corresponding text in either the JPEG (.JPG) or GIF89a file formats. The finished result will give you smooth text pop-ups when you attach a JavaScript to your buttons and roll over each button with the cursor in your browser.

You can view and try out these rollovers in Netscape Navigator or Microsoft Explorer, by opening the file popups.html in the WebMagic2/ Part IV folder on the CD-ROM. ∎

If you're creating Shockwave movies or using JavaScript to make your buttons move when you roll over or click them, then you'll really like these simple, 3D "clickable" button sequences! (You can find more information about using JavaScripts and Shockwave in Part V, "Tools.")

1 Create a new file (32×32, white). Set the foreground color to a medium color (I used a deep orange-red). Now create a new layer (Layer 1). Then using the elliptical Marquee tool, draw a circle centered in the middle of the image area. (Holding down (Option-Shift)[Alt-Shift] will help to make a perfectly round selection from the cursor insertion point.) Fill the selection with the foreground color.

2 Choose the Airbrush tool (10% opacity, 35-pixel soft-edged brush) and set the foreground color to white. Carefully airbrush an area in the upper left edge (10:00 position) of the circle to create a highlight area for the sphere. Continue by setting the foreground color to black, and airbrushing a small amount along the bottom edge (4:00 position) as shown here.

3 Choose Select➡Modify➡ Contract (five pixels). Then, choose Select➡Feather (one pixel), copy to the clipboard, and paste. This will position the clipboard contents on a new layer directly over the center of the sphere.

4 Choose Layer➡Transform➡ Rotate 180°. Notice how it instantly makes it look as though the button was being pushed in or indented!

5 Load the transparency selection for Layer I and choose Select➡ Modify➡Expand (two pixels). Then choose Select➡Feather (two pixels). Create a new layer (Layer 3) just above the background layer and fill the selection with black. Deselect the selection. You can adjust the positioning of this layer to suit your needs—whether it's to make the button appear as if it's embedded into the background or offset it down and to the right to create a drop shadow effect. Export the frames (both up and down sequences) in the GIF89a or JPEG(JPG) file formats.

VARIATIONS

You can use any background texture you like with this button to make it customized for your web page design.

Open the background tile texture file you are using for your web page (I used the Maple tile found in the WebMagic2/Part I folder on the CD-ROM). Choose Select➡All then Edit➡Define Pattern. Return to your button file and make the Background layer active. Fill the selection with the Pattern (100%, Normal). Export frames accordingly.

Here I created a metallic look. Make Layer I active and choose Image➡Adjust➡Hue/Saturation (Colorize, Hue: -120, Saturation: 20, Lightness: 0). Repeat with Layer 2. You can change the color of your buttons by adjusting these numbers...and see how many possibilities there are with this button design! ■

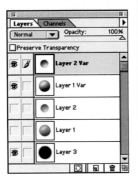

This animation effect will really get their attention. The type flies into the frame quickly, recoils to a sharp stop, then snaps right out of frame again, and continues in a loop. All of this great animation is only about 22K when it's compiled in the animated GIF format, so it loads fast too!

1 Create a new file (420×32, white). Set the foreground color to red. Insert text using the Type tool and center your text (Layer 1) in the middle of the image area (approximately 24-point type, depending on the font used). This will be your original type layer.

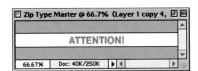

2 Duplicate Layer 1 (Layer 1 copy) and make Layer 1 invisible. Choose Filter➡Blur➡Motion Blur (Angle: 0, Distance: seven pixels). This will create the effect of fast horizontal motion.

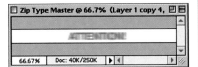

3 Make Layer 1 copy invisible. Duplicate Layer 1 (Layer 1 copy 2), choose Layer➡Transform➡Skew, and drag the top of the transform box to the left about 30 degrees as shown.

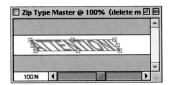

4 Choose Filter➡Blur➡Motion Blur (Angle: 0, Distance: seven pixels). This will give the effect of fast, blurred motion between frames.

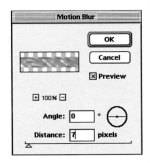

5 Make Layer 1 copy 2 invisible. Duplicate Layer 1 (Layer 1 copy 3) and choose Layer➡Transform➡ Skew. Drag the top of the transform box to the right about 45

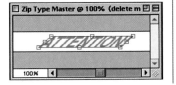

degrees as shown. Then choose Filter➥Blur➥Motion Blur (Angle: 0, Distance: seven pixels). This will create the illusion of "recoil" from stopping suddenly mid-frame.

6 Create a new layer (Layer 2) on top, and fill the layer with white, 100%. Move the new layer to the top of the Layers palette. Then choose the rectangular Marquee tool with the Feather set to 10 pixels and drag out the center section of the layer (approximately 80%) and delete as shown. This will give the edges of the animation a nice smooth entry and exit from the screen, by moving behind these soft transparent ends. Deselect the selection and hide all type layers, leaving a blank white image and the top fade layer. Export as frame 01, using the GIF 89a file format.

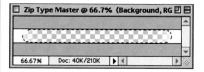

7 Make Layer 1 copy 3 active. Selecting the Move tool, move the layer to the left, and almost half out of the image window as shown. Export as frame 02.

 Holding down the shift key when moving a layer from side to side will keep in a clean, straight horizontal plane, so your animation will be smooth.

8 Repeat Step 7 for about three frames, moving Layer 1 copy 3 slightly to the right, ending up in the middle of the image area (at frame 05 of the animation). Make Layers 1, 1 copy 2 and 1 copy 3 active, adjusting the opacity of the layers to view the three layers' alignment. Adjust each layer with the Move tool so they are lined up centered horizontally, as shown here.

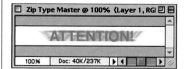

Zip Type Master @ 66.7% (Layer 1 copy 4,

66.67%   Doc: 40K/252K

9 Make all type layers invisible except for Layer 1 copy 3. Export as frame 06. Make Layer 1 copy invisible and make Layer 1 copy 3 visible. Export as frame 07. Continue by making Layer 1 copy 3 invisible and making Layer 1 copy visible. Export as frame 08. Then make Layer 1 copy invisible and make Layer 1 visible; export as frame 09. Make Layer 1 invisible, make Layer 1 copy 2 3 visible and export as frame 10. Then, using the Move tool, move it to the right and export frames 11, 12, and 13, similarly in distance to the first steps, ending-up with the image about halfway out of frame, as shown.

Zip Composite @ 75% (RGB)

		Frame #1
		Frame #2
		Frame #3
		Frame #4
		Frame #5
		Frame #6
		Frame #7
		Frame #8
Frame #9	ATTENTION!	
Frame #10		
Frame #11		
Frame #12		
Frame #13		

75%   Doc: 586K/391K

10 When building your animation, refer to the placement and alignment chart in this figure to get the best results. Notice how the type jumps "forward" just before coming to a stop in the middle. This will give the type a cartoon sort of feel, enforcing the illusion of speed and inertia on the animation. Then loop this animation in your GIF animation application, so the viewer can watch it several times.

You can view this animation with Netscape Navigator or Microsoft Explorer, by opening the file "zip-type.html" in the WebMagic2/Part IV folder on the CD-ROM. ■

PART V

Tools

Here's where the rubber meets the road! Animations and interactive rollovers and click-downs are really slick on your web site, but they take a little work to be fully functional. Creating the graphic sequences is the first step. Making things move, animate, interact, click, whatever—you'll need to master these utilities and techniques.

The tools briefly outlined in this section will help you successfully deliver the hard work you put into creating the cool graphics and animations from this book. From GIF animations to rollover scripts, basic web page layouts to fully interactive buttons with sound—familiarity with these tools will have you out from "under the hood" and in the driver's seat in no time!

Now let's dig in and get our hands dirty!

GIF Animator is a Windows-only shareware application for creating animated GIFs. In this application, you can create loops, transitions, and timed sequencing; adjust speed and direction; and so on. You can learn more about GIF Animator using its online help from the application. For this example, we'll create a loop sequence.

I Open GIF Animator and set your global information. These will be the settings that you want applied to the entire image, such as palette, looping options, and background color. Here only the background color gets changed.

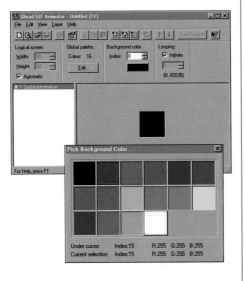

2 The easiest way to get your image sequences into the document is to open the window containing the images, select them all, and drag them into the list window on the left as shown. The images will automatically import in the order they are named alphabetically and the preview window will show you the images as they load. I used the Embossed Text animation sequence that is listed in the Animation section of the book, (as well as in the WebMagic2/Part IV folder on the *Photoshop Web Magic, Volume 2* CD-ROM).

3 When I created this animation, I didn't make all the frames needed to loop it. The animation only shows the text popping up out of the background. To make it go back down into the background is simply a matter of duplicating several frames and reversing their order. The first and last frames won't be duplicated because they will be the "start" and "stop" points of the animation.

4 Move each frame into position after it has been duplicated to create the reverse order sequence. Simply click and drag in the image file name window. Then click the preview button to see your animation in action. Save your completed animated GIF file and place into your HTML doc as you would any other GIF or JPEG file.

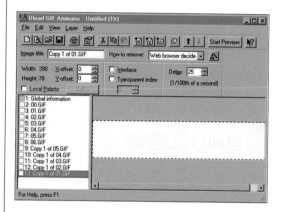

5 For more information and instructions on how to get the most out of GIF Animator, use the online Help utility. It's thorough and even has a step-by-step tutorial to follow!

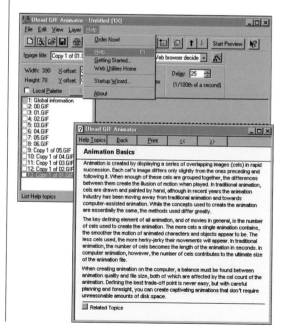

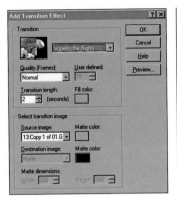

6 One of the many cool features of GIF Animator is its custom transitions feature. Here you can select transitions from one image to another with effects like wipes, window blinds, pushes, cubes, and so on.

You can find the GIF Animator shareware utility in the Software folder on the CD-ROM. Don't forget to register your product and pay the shareware fee so that you can keep using it! ■

GIF Builder is a Mac-only freeware application from Yves Piguet for creating animated GIFs. This is a very user-friendly utility that allows many on-the-fly choices like transitions, speed, looping, offset, image size, background colors, and so on. You can learn more about GIF Builder with its provided documentation. For this example, we'll create a loop sequence.

1 Open GIF Builder. Locate the folder with your animated image sequences in it (in this example, I use the Zip In-n-Out Type sequence from the Animation section of this book, as well as the WebMagic2/Part IV folder on the CD-ROM). Select all of the images and drag them into the Frames window. This will automatically place them in sequence and provide a preview window as they load.

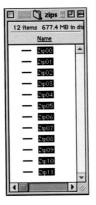

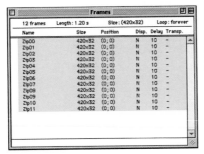

2 In this animation, I want the type to appear that it's coming to an abrupt stop, then zooming off to the right again. I select the clear, unblurred text frame, and adjust the Interframe Delay to slow it down at this point.

3 Choose Options➡Interframe Delay and set the speed up or down to your desired speed.

4 Next we'll loop the animation. Since I want this to animate indefinitely, I'm selecting Options➡Loop (Forever), but you can choose to have the animation loop any number of times and then stop on the last frame.

5 You can add more frames to smooth out the animation by duplicating the individual frames (choose Edit➡Duplicate Selection) and rearranging them by dragging them in the Frames window as shown.

You can find the GIF Builder freeware utility in the Software folder on the CD-ROM. Thank you, Yves, for making such a cool utility free for all of us to enjoy! ■

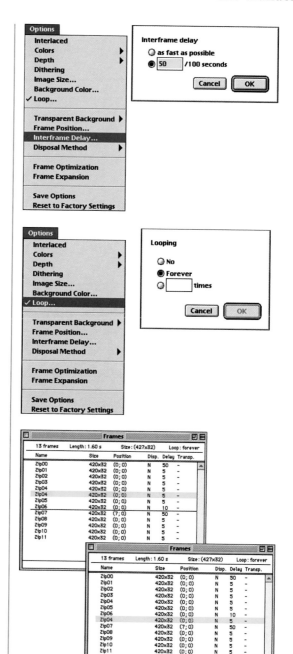

193

Claris HomePage 2.0

Claris Home Page is a WYSIWYG (What You See Is What You Get) HTML editor that enables you to create a web page with a fraction of the effort of writing the raw code. There is a 60-day free demo version of Home Page in the Software folder on the CD-ROM for you to evaluate. Many of the techniques and animation examples are quickly and easily imported into Home Page and previewed with Netscape in minutes. This isn't intended as a guide to the program but is just a few shortcuts to try-out some of your work quickly.

I Here's a quick reference of the Home Page Toolbar, for both Mac and Windows versions.

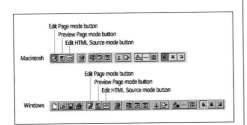

Open Home Page and click the Document Options button, bringing up the Options dialog box.

2 You can choose to change the global colors of your page at this point, including the type and background, as well as many other options. Here, I've selected white as my background color with the color palette.

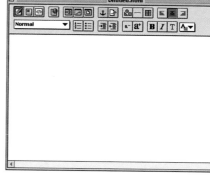

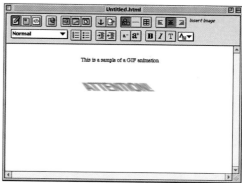

3 Inserting an image is as easy as clicking a single button. Here, I'm inserting an animated GIF file. Since the first frame of the animation is pure white, it doesn't show up here. The animation will not be running while in Home Page.

4 The final result is shown in the Netscape browser window, by simply clicking the Preview in Browser button.

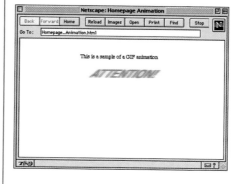

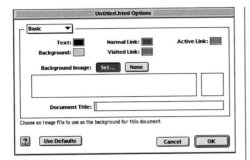

5 Adding a background texture tile is as simple as setting the color. Open the Document Options dialog box and click the Set Background Image button.

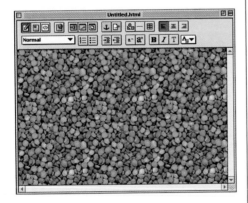

Select the image you want and it will appear in the background. Here, I used the Split Peas Tile in the WebMagic2/Part I/tiles folder on the CD-ROM.

6 You can easily access the online help by using the Help pull-down menu, which will guide you through several topics. ■

One of the biggest buzzwords in the web world these days is "Javascript." The most practical use of Javascript that I've seen is in the programming of image map hotspots or button "rollovers," which is when your cursor rolls over the hotspot or graphic, another image appears instantly (such as a down-button or glowing light).

In this example, I'm creating a simple single-image button rollover, using the Rocker Switch in the WebMagic2/Part III folder on the CD-ROM. You can also get the rollover script text file in the WeMagic2/Part IV folder on the CD-ROM, so you can simply cut and paste the script into your HTML doc. Let's take a closer look at the JavaScript and see how it works. This makes it easier for you to modify it for your own needs.

1 This first section of the Javascript states that there is a Javascript embedded. It also states which image(s) will be active upon loading. In this case, we will only be loading the two "on/off" rocker switch GIFs (sw1on.gif and sw1off.gif).

```
rollover.html

<HTML>
<HEAD>
<TITLE>Rollover Sample</TITLE>
<SCRIPT LANGUAGE = "JavaScript">

    if (document.images) {
        img1on = new Image();
        img1on.src = "sw1on.gif";

        img1off = new Image();
        img1off.src = "sw1off.gif";
    }

function imgOn(imgName) {
    if (document.images) {
        document[imgName].src = eval(imgName + "on.src");
    }
}

function imgOff(imgName) {
```

2 This next section is to activate the image files (when you roll onto the graphic).

```
        img1off = new Image();
        img1off.src = "sw1off.gif";
    }

function imgOn(imgName) {
    if (document.images) {
        document[imgName].src = eval(imgName + "on.src");
    }
}

function imgOff(imgName) {
    if (document.images) {
        document[imgName].src = eval(imgName + "off.src");
    }
}

</SCRIPT>
</HEAD>
<BODY BGCOLOR = "#000000">
<CENTER>
```

3 This next section is to de-activate the image files (when you roll off of the graphic). This is also where we will end the script statement.

```
function imgOn(imgName) {
    if (document.images) {
        document[imgName].src = eval(imgName + "on.src");
    }
}

function imgOff(imgName) {
    if (document.images) {
        document[imgName].src = eval(imgName + "off.src");
    }
}

</SCRIPT>
</HEAD>
<BODY BGCOLOR = "#000000">
<CENTER>
<BR>
<A HREF = "rolls2.html"
onMouseOver = "imgOn('img1')"
```

4 This section of the Javascript does several things with a few short commands. First, a URL is referenced, which means that when you click that graphic, you go directly to that document. The commands for the rollover, or "mouseOver/ mouseOut," which reference back to the JavaScript, follow. Finally, the actual image dimensions and referenced image name is called for.

```
function imgOff(imgName) {
    if (document.images) {
        document[imgName].src = eval(imgName + "off.src");
    }
}

</SCRIPT>
</HEAD>
<BODY BGCOLOR = "#000000">
<CENTER>
<BR>
<A HREF = "rolls2.html"
onMouseOver = "imgOn('img1')"
onMouseOut = "imgOff('img1')">
<IMG NAME= "img1" BORDER = 0 HEIGHT = 64 WIDTH = 32 SRC =
"sw1off.gif"></A>

</CENTER>
</BODY>
</HTML>
```

199

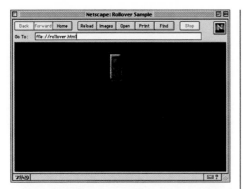

5 This is what it looks like in Netscape Navigator, both with the cursor on and off the button!

VARIATIONS

To use the same graphic image in several places on your page, but have separate rollovers and URL links, requires modifying your code slightly. This works especially well when you want to have a list with several repeating buttons or lights that glow when you rollover them.

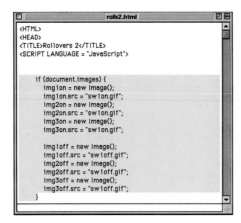

```
<HTML>
<HEAD>
<TITLE>Rollovers 2</TITLE>
<SCRIPT LANGUAGE = "JavaScript">


    if (document.images) {
        img1on = new Image();
        img1on.src = "sw1on.gif";
        img2on = new Image();
        img2on.src = "sw1on.gif";
        img3on = new Image();
        img3on.src = "sw1on.gif";

        img1off = new Image();
        img1off.src = "sw1off.gif";
        img2off = new Image();
        img2off.src = "sw1off.gif";
        img3off = new Image();
        img3off.src = "sw1off.gif";
    }
```

First, duplicate the two lines for "img1on," changing only the number 2 for the image callout as shown. (Make sure that you don't change the name of your "image1on.gif" files, or it won't be calling out for the same image.) Repeat this for as many repetitions of the rollover button you wish to be on the page. Continue the process with the "img1off" lines as shown.

Make a reference section for each rollover button instance on your page, making sure that the image callouts (img1, img2, and so on) don't conflict, and that each time the actual image is referenced, it remains the same name as the original as shown.

This might take a few trial and error attempts until you get the hang of it, but study the code here carefully and you will see the similarities and differences that will make sense to you eventually. Hey, whoever said that programming code made sense?

The result will be several independent rollover buttons using the same graphics, making loading the web page extremely fast and lean.

You can get more information about Javascript and other cool HTML tips and tricks from *HTML Web Magic* and *Java Web Magic* from Hayden Books. ■

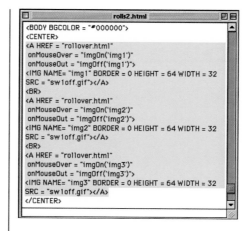

```
rolls2.html
<BODY BGCOLOR = "#000000">
<CENTER>
<A HREF = "rollover.html"
 onMouseOver = "imgOn('img1')"
 onMouseOut = "imgOff('img1')">
<IMG NAME= "img1" BORDER = 0 HEIGHT = 64 WIDTH = 32
SRC = "sw1off.gif"></A>
<BR>
<A HREF = "rollover.html"
 onMouseOver = "imgOn('img2')"
 onMouseOut = "imgOff('img2')">
<IMG NAME= "img2" BORDER = 0 HEIGHT = 64 WIDTH = 32
SRC = "sw1off.gif"></A>
<BR>
<A HREF = "rollover.html"
 onMouseOver = "imgOn('img3')"
 onMouseOut = "imgOff('img3')">
<IMG NAME= "img3" BORDER = 0 HEIGHT = 64 WIDTH = 32
SRC = "sw1off.gif"></A>
</CENTER>
```

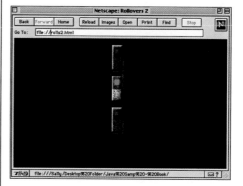

Shockwave is a technology developed by Macromedia that enables you to use Director with the Afterburner Xtra to create an interactive movie that can be "shocked" for use on the web. The nice part about a Shockwave animation is that it can be as small as a button and have full interactivity, including sound, music, and multiple animation sequence events.

This exercise will be using a simple one-click button with a single sound, which we will be able to import into a web page. A working knowledge of Macromedia Director and Lingo scripting is necessary to complete this exercise, but you can try out the finished Shockwave file in the WebMagic2/Part V folder on the CD-ROM.

I With the button movie open in Director, I check to see what size the cast member is, by double-clicking on it and reading the size values. This way I can set the Stage size to roughly the same size.

Bitmap Cast Member Properties

	Dial	OK
		Script...
	Options: ☐ Highlight When Clicked	Cancel
2 : Dial Internal	Color Depth: 16 bits	
	Palette: System - Mac ▼	
57 x 56 Size : 6.2 K	Unload: 3 - Normal ▼	Help

2 Using the Properties menu, set the Stage size slightly larger than the button cast member. You must keep it in increments of 16 pixels, because the Stage will "snap" to the closest size when you close the dialog box, and may crop your image area too tightly.

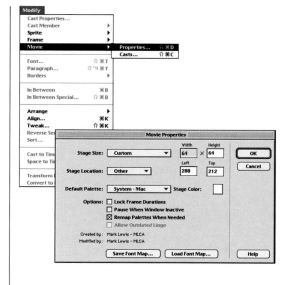

3 Placing the cast member into the score directly centers it correctly inside the Stage. In this example, I use a LegalButtonHandler Movie Script (found in the WebMagic2/Part V folder on the CD-ROM) that searches the cast palette for required "down button" sequence and sounds.

4 After your button is working properly, you're ready to create your Shockwave movie. Select the Afterburner Xtra from the Xtras menu and save your .dcr file. (If you don't have the Afterburner Xtra, you can get it at Macromedia's web site, located at: http://www.macromedia.com). That's it! Now you're ready to embed it into your HTML doc.

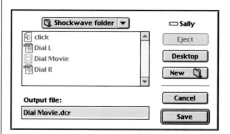

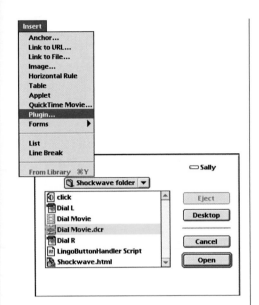

5 Using Claris Home Page, you can embed Shockwave files easily, by choosing Insert➡Plugin. Just select the file you want embedded.

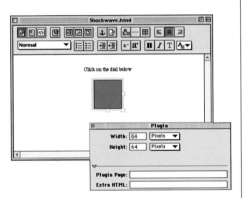

6 Sometimes the files don't come in at the correct size or proportions that you created the Shockwave file with. Make sure to check the dimensions of the file before you quit Director. You can check that they're correct by double-clicking the red "proxy" box to bring up the plug-in dialog box. Insert the correct sizes.

7 Click the Preview button and your page will open up in Netscape Navigator (or Microsoft Explorer, depending on your preferences), complete with working Shockwave button, provided you have the current Shockwave plug-ins in your browser.

You can get more information about Shockwave and other Macromedia products from their web site. ■

Appendix A

Web Resources

HTML pages containing these links can be found in the WebMagic2 folder on the CD. I've made every effort to supply the most up-to-date URLs available, but things are always changing, moving, and being removed from the web.

Information SuperLibrary

```
http://www.mcp.com
```

Viacom's Information SuperLibrary contains the complete text of *The Internet Starter Kit* (both Windows and Mac versions). Overall, the site contains the depth of information you would expect from the world's largest publisher of computer books.

Photoshop Resources

Adobe

```
http://www.adobe.com
```

The Adobe site contains continuing product support information, Photoshop and design tips, updates, plug-ins, and other up-to-date information.

Adobe Plug-In Source Catalog

```
http://www.imageclub.com/aps/
```

The Adobe Plug-in Source is a comprehensive software catalog that brings the power of plug-ins to your workstation.

216 Colors of Netscape

```
http://www.connect.hawaii.com/hc/webmasters/Netscape.colors.html
```

This is the place to learn about using the 216-color safe palette on the web.

Metacreations—KPT Plug-ins

```
http://www.metacreations.com
```

The developers of Kai's Power Tools, Kai's Power Goo, and other very cool graphics software.

PNG (Portable Network Graphics) Home Page

http://www.wco.com/~png/

Find out more about the PNG graphic format here.

Pantone: What's New

http://www.pantone.com/whatsnew.html

A great place for color resources, information, and software.

Design Resources

Designers Guide to the Net

http://www.zender.com/designers-guide-net

This site, and the book it is based on, attempt to raise the right questions, and propose answers that will help designers in the information future.

Pursuing Page Publishing

http://www.links.net/webpub/

Tips on "Publish yo' self" at this site. Includes a guide to designing with HTML and links to many other web resources.

Cybergrrl

http://www.cybergrrl.com

Author of *Designing Web Graphics*, Lynda Weinman's Cybergrrl site helps guide you through getting started on the web, offers HTML instruction, links you to important web sites, and lots more.

Web Wonk—Tips for Writers and Designers

http://www.dsiegel.com/tips/index.html

Web Wonk by David Siegel, author of *Creating Killer Web Sites*, will help you to build better web pages, use email, and offers great tips on Web site graphic design.

Tom's Tips for Web Designers

http://shiva.snu.ac.kr/KPT/Toms/

Find all kinds of Photoshop tips here including: web design, using filters, and links to other resources.

Ventana: Photoshop f/x

http://www.vmedia.com/vvc/onlcomp/phshpfx/

This site, based on the book *Photoshop f/x*, has lots of design tips and links to Photoshop resources.

Yahoo Design and Layout

http://www.yahoo.com/Computers_and_Internet/Internet/World_Wide_Web/Page_Design_and_Layout

This Yahoo category is as up to date and comprehensive as it gets. It includes links to Animated GIFs, Backgrounds, Color Information, Commercial Books, Commercial Web Pages, Designers, HTML, Icons, Imagemaps, Programming, Transparent Images, and Validation/Check.

Backgrounds

Texture Land—Abnormal Textures Index

http://www.meat.com/textures/aindex.html

This site offers one of the largest selections of backgrounds on the web.

KALEIDESCAPE

http://www.steveconley.com/kaleid.htm

This site claims to offer "hundreds of the snazziest textures in the universe."

Textures Unlimited!

http://stega.smoky.org/~bzhuk/

Click on a texture at this site and it automatically shows you what the tile looks like when applied to a web page. There are some flashy textures here and music clips to download.

Greg's Texture Tiles Page

http://mars.ark.com/~gschorno/tiles/

Find lots of tiles here in a simple table-based layout.

The Background Sampler

http://www.netscape.com/assist/net_sites/bg/backgrounds.html

Netscape's collection of backgrounds. Lots of basic textures and standard patterns here.

The Wallpaper Machine

http://www.cacr.caltech.edu/cgi-bin/wallpaper.pl

This interactive page makes funky random background patterns each time you click Reload.

Netscape—Color Backgrounds

http://home.netscape.com/assist/net_sites/bg/

Netscape's instruction page on using background color with HTML3.

InfiNet's Background Colors List

http://www.infi.net/wwwimages/colorindex.html

Information on setting and using hex color for web page backgrounds and text.

Vicious Fishes—Free Stuff!

http://www.viciousfishes.com/freestuff.html

Free to download theme-oriented backgrounds, rules, boxes, and more.

Type on the Web

TypoGraphic

http://www.razorfish.com/bluedot/typo/

This site is meant to illustrate the beauty, poetry, complexity, and history of type, while raising relevant questions about how typography is treated in the digital media, specifically online.

DesktopPublishing.com

http://desktoppublishing.com/

Lots of fonts, images, and links to a wide range of design and programming resources.

Type Directors Club

http://members.aol.com/typeclub/index.html

An organization dedicated to the appreciation and understanding of letterforms and calligraphy.

BitStream Fonts

http://www3.digitalriver.com/bit/

Over 1,000 fonts for sale online.

Letraset

http://www.letraset.com/letraset/

Download a free sample font, review new fonts, plus clip art and stock photography.

Coolfont

http://members.aol.com/fontdude/coolfont.htm

If you are into grunge and other trendy types of fonts, Fontdude's site offers a great collection for a modest fee.

Buttons

Welcome to the WebTools Home Page

http://www.artbeatswebtools.com/frdoor.html

Artbeats WebTools is a CD-ROM containing hundreds of web page elements: buttons, headings, rules, and so on. Download sample images here.

Art and Sound Bites™—Vol. 1

http://www.viciousfishes.com

A series of customizable, theme-oriented "interface kits," including backgrounds, buttons, mortises, windows and sounds—perfect for Shockwave or Java! Download kit component samples here.

Download Free Clip Art

http://www.sausage.com/clipart.htm

The folks at Sausage Software, makers of the Hot Dog Pro HTML editor, offer some very nice textures, clip art, and buttons for your pages.

Button World

http://www.demon.co.uk/Tangent/buttons.html

Button World is a collection of blank buttons, each one optimized for rapid transmission over the Internet. Add text to these buttons and use them on your web pages.

Clip Art

Double-exposure Home Page Starter Kit

http://www.doubleexposure.com

Icons, buttons, clip art—order collections from this site or download and use some of the sample images they offer.

Metatoys
http://metatoys.metatools.com

Search through over 2,200 images from the Power Photos and MetaPhotos collections online, then purchase and download just the images you want for immediate use.

Ulead Systems Multimedia Solutions
http://www.ulead.com/

Makers of GIF Animator and lots of other cool stuff for Windows.

Publishers Depot
http://www.publishersdepot.com/

This site calls itself a one-stop site for digital photography, fonts, video, and audio. It pretty much lives up to its claim with thousands of images and resources to choose from.

Photodisc
http://www.photodisc.com/

Simply the largest collection of royalty free, digital stock photography on the Internet.

Animation Resources

1st Internet Gallery of GIF Animation
http://members.aol.com/royalef/galframe.htm

This is one of the best starting points for information on GIF animation resources, samples, and technical information.

Java Programming Resources

http://www.apl.jhu.edu/~hall/java/

Java samples, animations, and lots of links and resources.

The Web—Getting Started

CERN—Where the Web Was Developed
http://www.cern.ch/

CERN, European Laboratory for Particle Physics, is where the web was developed. The WWW Support Team runs the main WWW server at CERN and gives general support.

The World Wide Web Consortium
```
http://www.w3.org/
```

W3C is an industry consortium which develops common standards for the evolution of the web by producing specifications and reference software.

InterNIC Domain Registration Services
```
http://www.internic.net
```

The InterNIC is the primary source for domain registration. You can do a search here for names that aren't already taken.

The List—Internet Service Providers
```
http://www.thelist.com/
```

Get information on over 3,000 ISPs (Internet Service Providers). Listed geographically and by area code.

c/net Guide to ISPs
```
http://www.cnet.com/Content/Reviews/Compare/ISP/
```

Tips on how to choose an ISP along with vital statistics on national and local ISPs. Find out which ISPs live up to their claims, and which you should be wary of until they clean up their act.

WPD–Magazine Rack
```
http://www.littleblue.com/webpro/magazinerack.html
```

The Web Professionals' Digest–Magazine Rack links you to over 75 web-based, web-focused magazines.

A Beginner's Guide to URLs
```
http://www.ncsa.uiuc.edu/demoweb/url-primer.html
```

What is a URL? A URL is a Uniform Resource Locator. This beginner's guide offers a quick walk through of some of the more common URL types and how to use them.

Beginner's Guide to HTML
```
http://www.ncsa.uiuc.edu/General/Internet/WWW/HTMLPrimer.html
```

This is the most requested page on the National Center for Supercomputing Applications (NCSA) Web site. If you are interested in learning HTML this is the starting point.

211

Glenn's Cheat Sheet on HTML Style

```
http://info.med.yale.edu/caim/StyleManual_Top.HTML
```

Learn HTML directly from Yale's Center for Advanced Instructional Media. This site contains concise HTML instructions and tips.

Submit It

```
http://submit-it.permalink.com/submit-it/
```

Once you have your site up on the web you will need to get it listed on search engines, and so on. One of the best places to do this is at Submit It.

AAA Internet Promotions

```
http://www.websitepromote.com/
http://www.west.net/~solution/
```

More than just search engine submissions, this company has several targeted Internet marketing programs for any size company and budget.

Web Resources

Shareware.com

```
http://www.shareware.com
```

If it's shareware, you can find it here. Over 200,000 searchable, downloadable software files.

TUCOWS

```
http://www.tucows.com
```

The Ultimate Collection Of Winsock Software—with mirror sites all over the world, you can find the latest and greatest shareware and freeware tools for both Mac and Windows here.

Bandwidth Conservation Society

```
http://www.infohiway.com/faster
```

This site is a resource to help web page designers with an interest in optimizing performance, while maintaining an appropriate graphic standard. Information on file formats, links to Java applets, and more.

BrowserWatch

`http://browserwatch.iworld.com`

Go to this site to keep up on the latest news on browsers, plug-ins, and other web resources.

EFF—The Electronic Frontier Foundation

`http://www.eff.org/`

The EFF is an important organization helping to keep the web free from censorship.

JavaWorld—Java Jumps

`http://www.javaworld.com/common/jw-jumps.html`

This is a comprehensive collection of links to Java resources, collections, tools, and so on.

Shockwave—Macromedia Shockzone

`http://www.macromedia.com/shockzone/`

Everything Shockwavable—including free plug-ins to download, information on Shockwave and Flash 2.

The VRML Repository

`http://www.sdsc.edu/vrml`

The VRML Repository is an impartial, comprehensive, community resource for the dissemination of information relating to VRML. Maintained by the San Diego Supercomputer Center (SDSC).

The Perl Language Home Page

`http://www.perl.com/perl/index.html`

Learn about Perl, a common CGI language, with over 5,000 Perl resources and CGI's.

CGI Test Cases

`http://hoohoo.ncsa.uiuc.edu/cgi/examples.html`

A collection of CGI's to add forms, animation, functionality, and more to your web pages.

Appendix B

Contributors Listing

Software and Filters

Adobe Systems, Inc.

345 Park Avenue

San Jose, CA 95110-6000

Phone: 408-536-6000

Fax: 408-537-6000

http://www.adobe.com

Acrobat Reader® 3.0 (Mac and PC)

Photoshop® 4.0.1 Tryout (Mac and PC)

After Effects™ 3.1 Tryout (Mac and PC)

Streamline™ 4.0 Tryout (Mac and PC)

Dimensions® 3.0 Tryout (Mac and PC)

Illustrator®7.0 Tryout (Mac and PC)

Alien Skin Software

1100 Wake Forest Rd. Suite 101

Raleigh, NC 27604 USA

Phone: 919-832-4124

Fax: 919-832-4065

http://www.alienskin.com

Eye Candy 3.0 Demo (Mac and PC)

Claris

5201 Patrick Henry Drive

Santa Clara, CA 95052

http://www.claris.com

Claris Home Page 2.0 Demo (Mac and PC)

Macromedia, Inc.

600 Townsend Street

San Francisco, CA 94103

Phone: 415-252-2000

Fax: 415-626-0554

http://www.macromedia.com

Director® 6 demo (Mac and PC)

MetaTools, Inc.

6303 Carpinteria Ave.

Carpinteria, CA 93013

Phone: 805-566-6200

metasales@aol.com

KPT 3.0 Demo (Mac and PC)

Ulead Systems Inc.

970 West 190th Street, Suite 520

Torrance, CA 90502

Phone: 310-523-9393

Fax: 310-523-9399

info@ulead.com

http://www.ulead.com

GIF Animator (PC only)

Vicious Fishes Software

530 E. Lambert Rd.

Brea, CA 92821

Phone: 714-671-0330

Fax: 714-671-2871

fdi@viciousfishes.com

http://www.viciousfishes.com

Demo of Art and Sound Bites, Vol. 1

Xaos Tools, Inc

55 Hawthorn Suite 1000

San Francisco, CA 94105

Phone: 800-BUY-XAOS

http://www.xaostools.com/profile.html

Paint Alchemy 2™ Demo (Mac only)

Terrazo 2™ Demo (Mac only)

TypeCaster™ Demo (Mac only)

Yves Piguet

piguet@ia.epfl.ch

http://iawww.epfl.ch/staff/yves.piguet

GIFBuilder (Mac only)

Stock Images

FotoSets

4104 24th St., #425

San Francisco, CA 94114

Phone: 415-621-2061

Fax: 415-621-2917

Image Club Graphics

729 24th Ave. SE

Calgary, AB Canada

T2G 5K8

Phone: 403-262-8008 or 800-661-9410

Fax: 403-261-7013

http:www.adobe.com/imageclub

MetaTools, Inc.

6303 Carpinteria Ave.

Carpinteria, CA 93013

Phone: 805-566-6200

metasales@aol.com

PhotoDisc/CMCD

2013 Fourth Ave., 4th Floor

Seattle, WA 98121

Phone: 206-441-9355 or 800-528-3472

http://www.photodisc.com

Fonts

Delve Media Arts

P.O. Box 641053 (PC only)

San Francisco, CA 94164-1053

Phone: 415-474-0702

http://www.delvemediarts.com

delve@delvemediarts.com

Foundry Group

Jon Armstrong (Mac and PC)

c/o Foundry Group/Saiph Corporation

250 West 57th Street

New York, NY

Phone: 718-384-2583

jon@saiph.com

http://www.foundrygroup.com/

Ingrimayne Type

Robert Schenk (Mac and PC)

P.O. Box 404

Rensselaer, IN 47978

bobs@kagi.com

http://ingrimayne.saintjoe.edu/

Omnibus Typografi

Box 135 (Mac and PC)

S-135 23 Tyreso

Sweden

Phone: +46 8 742 8336

Fax: +46 8 712 3993

info@omnibus.se

http://www.omnibus.se

217

P22 Type Foundry

(Mac and PC)

P.O. Box 770 West Side Station

Buffalo, New York 14213-0070

Phone: 716-885-4490

Fax: 716-885-4482

p22@p22.com

http://www.p22.com

Three Islands Press

P.O. Box 442 (Mac and PC)

Rockland, ME 04841-0442

Phone: 207-596-6768

Fax: 207-596-7403

info@3ip.com

http://www.3ip.com

Vitatype Digital Fonts

5204 Hadley Court, #1 (PC only)

Overland Park, KS 66202

Phone: 913-677-2533

jeff@vitatype.com

http://www.primenet/~jeffib

Appendix C

What's on the CD-ROM

The CD-ROM that comes with this book is both Mac and Windows compatible. Samples, demos, and shareware applications are included that will help you create and follow along with the effects in this book with no frustration.

I suggest that you refer to the READ ME files and other help information accompanying the software demos and shareware applications on the disk. Also, visit a few web sites; the URLs are noted in Appendix A, "Web Resources." These web sites often contain demos of new software available for downloading and tryout.

The CD-ROM is divided into three folders:

WebMagic2

In this folder you will find all of the working web pages for each effect, as well as the ready-to-use backgrounds to follow along with. I've referred to the contents of this folder throughout the book for you to review sample animations and to get working files from, like the JavaScript file referred to in the Tools section. You will also find some examples of combining some of the techniques to create "themes" for continuity in your designs.

Filters

Some demos and sample Photoshop filters are included here from Alien Skin, MetaTools, and Xaos Tools, to enhance your designs even more. Have fun and experiment with these cool filters!

Software

This is where you will find the demo software mentioned in Part V, "Tools," which includes:

- Claris Home Page (Mac/Win 60 day trial version)
- GIF Animator (Win shareware demo)
- GIF Builder (Mac freeware)
- Assorted demos and working samples from Adobe, Macromedia, and Vicious Fishes.

Photoshop Web Magic, Volume 2

Gallery

Ghost Type Tile

page 28

Microbricks

page 30

Microtiles

page 32

Notebook

page 36

Organic Tiles

page 40

Photo Tiles

page 46

Relief Logos

page 50

Photoshop Web Magic, Volume 2

Buttons, Switches, and Arrows

Oval Buttons

page 90

3 D Arrows

page 92

Dial Switches

page 96

Glass Marbles

page 100

Metal Buttons

page 104

Plastic Bars

page 108

Rocker Switches

page 112

WATER TYPE

page 116

Type on Buttons

Animations

Banner Ads

Bouncing Ball

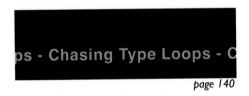

aaaaaaaaaaaaa
Embossed Type

Flying Arrows

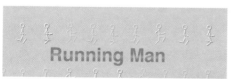

Running Man

Photoshop Web Magic, Volume 2

MACMILLAN COMPUTER PUBLISHING USA

A V I A C O M   C O M P A N Y

Technical

Support:

If you cannot get the CD/Disk to install properly, or you need assistance with a particular situation in the book, please feel free to check out the Knowledge Base on our Web site at **http://www.superlibrary.com/general/support**. We have answers to our most Frequently Asked Questions listed there. If you do not find your specific question answered, please contact Macmillan Technical Support at **(317) 581-3833**. We can also be reached by email at **support@mcp.com**.